Disruptive Behavior Disorders in Children

Disruptive Behavior Disorders in Children

Meredith Weber
Erica Burgoon

MP MOMENTUM PRESS
HEALTH

First published in 2017 by
Momentum Press®, LLC
222 East 46th Street, New York, NY 10017
www.momentumpress.net

ISBN-13: 978-1-94474-921-7 (print)
ISBN-13: 978-1-94474-922-4 (e-book)

Momentum Press Child Clinical Psychology "Nuts and Bolts" Collection

Cover and interior design by S4Carlisle Publishing Services Private Ltd., Chennai, India

First edition: 2017

10 9 8 7 6 5 4 3 2 1

Printed in the United States of America

Abstract

Children and teenagers who present with externalizing disorders, such as conduct disorder or impulse control disorder, can be incredibly challenging for their parents, teachers, and loved ones. The behaviors of these children can also be vexing for schools and other systems in which they are educated and treated. These children are at increased risk for being placed in more restrictive settings, including juvenile justice placements (Frick, Ray, Thornton, & Kahn, 2014a; Khanna, Shaw, Dolan, & Lennox, 2014). They are also at increased risk for adult criminal behavior and other negative outcomes (Khanna et al., 2014; Salekin, 2015).

There has long been debate and controversy over the best way to treat children with "acting out" or defiant behaviors, including whether or not these disorders should even be included in the DSM. Some "explosive children" are reacting to psychosocial and environmental stressors in the most adaptive ways they know, and others are acting out of other skill deficits while still others may be seeking stimulation, or struggling to manage impulses. Some children who act in antisocial ways are conceived as demonstrating early signs of psychopathy (Salekin, 2015).

Conduct disorders and the ways in which they are treated present a challenge not only for those in a child's life, but also for society as a whole. The practice of "zero tolerance" policies in schools, which began after highly publicized school shootings in the 1990s, is now being questioned, and educators and mental health professionals are looking to more effective approaches (National Association of School Psychologists [NASP], 2001; Skiba, 2000).

This volume will provide those who work with children a description of best practice in diagnosing and treating children with impulse control disorder and other disorders of conduct, including management of risk. It will also address what is evidence-based practice versus ill-informed policy so that those who work, live, and teach children with challenging behaviors can best help them succeed.

Keywords

Adolescents, Aggression, Behavior, Child Psychology, Children, Conduct Disorder, Conduct, Disruptive Behavior Disorders, Mental Health, Oppositional Defiant Disorder, Youth

Contents

Acknowledgments

The authors would like to thank Sam Gontkovsky for his invitation to contribute to this series and for his encouragement, guidance, and support, and Peggy Williams for her unending patience and support.

Thank you to the families and children with whom I have worked who have taught me about resilience and courage. I would like to acknowledge the invaluable help and support provided by my parents, Gail and Howard, sister Jessica and sister-in-law Nancy, in helping make this possible through their help with childcare during writing and support and encouragement through this process. My husband Jim was a constant source of support and encouragement before, during, and after this process. Finally, I'd like to thank my son Eli, for his great hugs and for being my inspiration always. —MW

I am grateful to many supervisors, mentors, and colleagues who have provided invaluable professional guidance and support throughout my training and career, and the families with whom I have had the privilege to work. Each has contributed to my professional growth and left me a better clinician for the next family. I would like to thank my husband Jonathan who tries, some days with more success than others, to help me stay level-headed. Most of all I would like to thank some of the most influential teachers I have ever had, my children Riley, Harper, and Kendall. —EB

CHAPTER 1

Description and Diagnosis

Children and teenagers who present with externalizing disorders, such as conduct disorder or impulse control disorder, can be incredibly challenging for their parents, teachers, and loved ones. The behaviors of these children can also be vexing for schools and other systems in which they are educated and treated. These children are at increased risk for being placed in more restrictive settings, including juvenile justice placements (Frick, Ray, Thornton, & Kahn, 2014a; Khanna, Shaw, Dolan, & Lennox, 2014). Disruptive Behavior Disorders represent the most common reason for referral to youth outpatient mental health services. In schools, aggression and problems with conduct make up the largest proportion of placements in special education classes (Dodge & Pettit, 2003).

They are also at increased risk for adult criminal behavior and other negative outcomes such as later substance abuse (Khanna et al., 2014; Salekin, 2015). Continued antisocial behavior as an adult is associated with diminished academic, social, and educational attainment, higher divorce and unemployment rates, and increased rates of incarceration (Frick, 2016). Additionally, the cost of these disorders to society can start adding up when one considers the costs of residential placement or incarceration, the costs associated with specific antisocial behaviors, such as theft, property destruction, and injury to others, decreased earnings over a lifetime, and other ways in which youth with disruptive behavior problems can end up on negative lifetime trajectories and as a result, not be in the labor market or contributing to a community tax base. The costs to society of children with disruptive behavior disorders have been estimated to account for a larger percentage of health care costs than children with chronic health conditions such as epilepsy, diabetes, and asthma (Guevara, Mandell, Rostain, Zhao, & Hadley, 2003). Fortunately, there are treatments that work, and these diagnoses do not need to lead to chronic behavior problems over one's lifetime if addressed quickly and treated appropriately.

One of the major changes to surround oppositional defiant disorder (ODD), conduct disorder, and impulse control disorder in the fifth and most recent edition of the *Diagnostic and Statistical Manual of Mental Disorders* (*DSM*) is that these disorders are now all in a new category titled "Disruptive, Impulse-Control, and Conduct Disorders" (American Psychiatric Association, 2013a, p. 461) that generally refer to conditions marked by behaviors that impact the rights of others (American Psychiatric Association, 2013a). Previously, they were part of a grouping called "Disorders Usually First Diagnosed in Infancy, Childhood, or Adolescence" and "Impulse Control Disorders Not Otherwise Specified" (American Psychiatric Association, 2013b).

1.1   Conduct Disorder

It is estimated that 8.5% of youth will meet criteria for conduct disorder at some point in their lives, with the majority of those diagnosed also being boys (Substance Abuse and Mental Health Services Administration [SAMHSA], 2015). A meta-analysis estimated that the worldwide prevalence of conduct disorder in children aged 6 to 18 years is thought to be around 3.2%, though it should be cautioned that the majority of the studies they looked at were from Western countries (Canino, Polanczyk, Bauermeister, Rohde, & Frick, 2010). The U.S. SAMHSA currently estimates that the prevalence of ODD is 3.3% in the United States, mostly consisting of boys. In the *DSM-5*, the prevalence is estimated at between 2% and 10% with a median of 4% for 1 year prevalence, with stable rates noted across various countries with heterogeneous populations (American Psychiatric Association, 2013). While conduct disorder is much more prevalent in boys, conduct and behavior problems remain the most frequent referral issues for mental health treatment for girls (Frick, 2016). The difference in prevalence in conduct disorders between girls and boys is less pronounced in young children under age five. By childhood, the incidence of conduct disorder in boys to girls is 3:2; by adolescence, the prevalence is 2:1 for boys to girls.

The *DSM-5* retains the same general diagnostic criteria for conduct disorder as the two preceding editions of the *DSM*, the *DSM-IV* (American Psychiatric Association, 1994) and *DSM-IV-TR* (American Psychiatric Association, 2000). These editions of the *DSM* describe conduct disorder as "A repetitive and persistent pattern of behavior in which the basic rights of others or major age-appropriate societal norms or rules are violated," as manifested by the presence of at least 3 of 15 criteria organized under the categories of Aggression to People and Animals, Destruction of Property, Deceitfulness or Theft, and Serious Violations of Rules. There is no diagnostic requirement that an individual meets the criteria from a designated number of categories; however, the diagnosis requires that the individual has exhibited at least three criteria in the preceding 12 months and at least one criterion in the preceding 6 months. Further, *DSM* diagnostic criteria include "The disturbance in behavior causes clinically significant impairment in social, academic, or occupational functioning" and "If the individual is age 18 years or older, criteria are not met for antisocial personality disorder" (American Psychiatric Association, 2013, p. 470).

Like the two preceding editions of the *DSM*, the *DSM-5* includes specifiers of childhood-onset type, appropriate for individuals who exhibited at least one symptom of conduct disorder prior to age 10, and adolescent-onset type, appropriate for individuals who did not exhibit symptoms of conduct disorder until age 10 or after. However, the *DSM-5* also includes a specifier of unspecified onset, appropriate for individuals for whom there is not adequate historical information to determine the age of symptom onset, which was not included in previous editions. Research has shown that individuals diagnosed with childhood-onset conduct disorder tend to display a more aggressive and severe pattern of disruptive behavior and have a poorer prognosis than those who did not begin exhibiting symptoms of conduct disorder until preadolescence or later (Frick, 2016; Lahey et al., 1999; McCabe, Hough, Wood & Yeh, 2001). Children who display signs of conduct disorder earlier in childhood are more likely to demonstrate related problems later in life, including a greater likelihood of meeting the criteria for antisocial personality disorder as in adulthood (Myers, Stewart & Brown, 1998) and higher incidence of criminal behavior (Moffit, Caspi, Dickson, Silva & Stanton,

1996). The *DSM-5* also retains specifiers to describe current symptom severity—mild, moderate, and severe.

The *DSM-5* contains a new specifier that did not appear in previous editions called *with limited prosocial emotions*. This specifier is listed if the individual has persistently displayed at least two of four characteristics over a 12-month period and in multiple settings—lack of remorse or guilt, callousness or lack of empathy, lack of concern about performance, and shallow or deficient affect. Because this specifier should only be used if the characteristics are typical of the person's functioning, rather than occasional displays of behavior, the *DSM-5* notes that it is necessary to gather information from multiple sources, including from those who have known the individual for an extended time and in multiple settings, to determine whether the individual meets the criteria for this specifier. The *DSM-5* notes, "Individuals with characteristics described in this specifier may be more likely than other individuals with conduct disorder to engage in aggression that is planned for instrumental gain" (American Psychiatric Association, 2013, p. 471). Instrumental aggression refers to aggression committed for a purpose, such as to obtain something, without concern for any consequences to the people harmed in the act, versus aggression committed as a way to communicate a need, or committed as self-defense to potential, real, or perceived harm to oneself. It is important for any clinician working with a child displaying disruptive behaviors to obtain as accurate an understanding of what purpose the behavior is serving and the circumstances around the behavior. A child, with a history of neglect, who routinely steals from others should not be diagnosed or treated in the same way as would a child who engages in theft for other reasons. Similarly, a child who steals small things as part of a compulsive disorder should not be viewed as being primarily conduct disordered in the absence of other types of conduct problems.

Historically, youth who would meet the criteria for limited prosocial emotions were often referred to as callous-unemotional, or having what is often referred to in the literature as "CU traits." The specifier of limited prosocial emotions is intended to provide information about level of clinical impairment or severity, as well as prognostic information, as there is evidence that youth who meet the criteria for this specifier may have a particularly limited response to typical interventions and require alternative treatment interventions (Frick, Ray, Thornton & Kahn, 2014b). Many clinicians perceive these youth to experience a heightened sense of satisfaction and enjoyment from their negative behavior and its consequences in comparison to other youth who engage in a pattern of negative behavior. Further, many clinicians perceive the drive to engage in negative behavior among these youth as something that is core to their personalities in comparison to youth whose conduct problems might be better understood in the context of factors such as poor problem solving or socially conditioned behavior. Some children who act in anti-social ways are conceived as demonstrating early signs of psychopathy (Salekin, 2015). While the term *psychopathy* has historically been used interchangeably with antisocial personality disorder, it is not a specific clinical diagnosis currently listed in the *DSM*. Rather, while the current diagnostic features of both antisocial personality disorder and conduct disorder focus on externally observable behavioral indicators, psychopathy has become recognized as a clinical concept that refers to a cluster of personality traits that are typically present over the life span. In many individuals with antisocial personality disorder or conduct disorder, psychopathic personality traits underlie or drive the types of behaviors that lead to the diagnosis of these disorders, including grandiosity, callousness, lack of empathy and remorse, and shallow affect (Hare, 1993). However, not all youth with conduct disorder or other disruptive behavior disorders have psychopathy and there are other explanations for the development of disruptive behavior in these youth.

1.2   Oppositional Defiant Disorder

Oppositional defiant disorder (ODD) is a diagnosis that first made its way into the *DSM* in 1980 with the *DSM-III* (American Psychiatric Association, 1980). Traditionally, it describes a child who is defiant and oppositional so frequently that it impedes the functioning of that child in the school, home, or other settings that are part of the child's life. In the *DSM-5*, the median prevalence of ODD is estimated at around 3.3% with the incidence being higher in males than females prior to adolescence; this difference in male predominance then goes away after adolescence (American Psychiatric Association, 2013).

In the most recent version of the DSM, oppositional defiant disorder is defined as:

> A pattern of angry/irritable mood, argumentative/defiant behavior, or vindictiveness lasting at least 6 months as evidenced by at least four symptoms from any of the following categories, and exhibited during interaction with at least one individual who is not a sibling.
>
> Angry/Irritable Mood:
>
> 1. Often loses temper.
> 2. Is often touchy or easily annoyed.
> 3. Is often angry and resentful.
>
> Argumentative/Defiant Behavior:
>
> 4. Often argues with authority figures or, for children and adolescents, with adults.
> 5. Often actively defies or refuses to comply with requests from authority figures or with rules.
> 6. Often deliberately annoys others.
> 7. Often blames others for his or her mistakes or misbehavior.
> 8. Vindictiveness
> 9. Has been spiteful or vindictive at least twice within the past 6 months.

(American Psychiatric Association, 2013, p. 462)

As one reads over the criteria, it becomes clear that any of these behaviors could be a part of the repertoire of a typical child. One of the updates to the diagnosis in this edition of the *DSM* is the caution to the reader to use persistence and frequency as a way to distinguish the above behaviors from behaviors that may be within typical limits for a given child, adding the specifiers, "For children younger than 5 years, the behavior should occur on most days for a period of at least 6 months unless otherwise noted (Criterion A8). For individuals 5 years or older, the behavior should occur at least once per week for at least 6 months, unless otherwise noted (Criterion A8)" (American Psychiatric Association, 2013, p. 462).

An additional note of caution is given by way of trying to distinguish clinical symptoms from what may be considered more appropriate responses in a child's culture and environment: "While these frequency criteria provide guidance on a minimal level of frequency to define symptoms, other factors should also be considered, such as whether the frequency and intensity of the behaviors are outside a range that is normative for the individual's developmental level, gender, and culture" (American Psychiatric Association, 2013, p. 462). Culture can play an essential role in that family expectations around what constitutes appropriate behavior, and appropriate communication with caregivers can vary widely. One meta-analysis found that families from Asia tolerated a lower level of externalizing behaviors than did families of Western descent (Canino et al., 2010). Understanding how individual differences and cultural expectations may or may not line up is not only an essential part of cultural competence but also of accurate diagnosis. Every family also has its own culture and set of experiences, and assessing individual family expectations is crucial to understanding whether or not a child's difficulties are best captured with a diagnosis of ODD.

An important change to the criteria for ODD from the last *DSM* is the removal of the exclusion criterion for conduct disorder. Previously, readers were cautioned that conduct disorder and ODD could not both be diagnosed at the same time, this is no longer true and now criteria for both disorders can be met at the same time.

1.3   Impulse Control and Intermittent Explosive Disorder

Children whose impulse control is impaired may often be conceptualized as having an underlying disorder of attention or executive function. Children who are diagnosed with attention deficit hyperactivity disorder (ADHD) often display symptoms of impulse control disorder. These children may struggle to inhibit their initial responses or desires and so may grab something they want when they know that they should not, or who may push a peer who has upset them without thinking through the consequences or without being able to heed any cautionary thoughts that this may be a bad idea. There have been demonstrable associations between poor impulse control and conduct disorder, with poorer developmental trajectories predicted for those children with conduct disorder, who also display impulsive symptoms (Ipser & Stein, 2007). There is a high level of comorbidity with conduct disorder and ADHD with an estimated 50% of youth referred for outpatient clinical services for ADHD also being diagnosed with conduct disorder (Ipser & Stein, 2007). One study found that children and adolescents diagnosed with conduct disorder were seven times more likely to be diagnosed with a comorbid impulse control disorder in the course of their lifetime than were children who did not meet criteria for conduct disorder (Nock, Kazdin, Hiripi, & Kessler, 2006).

The diagnosis of intermittent explosive disorder, which is now in the "Disruptive Behavior Disorders" category of the *DSM-5*, is characterized by:

Recurrent outbursts that demonstrate an inability to control impulses, including either of the following:

- Verbal aggression (tantrums, verbal arguments, or fights) or physical aggression that occurs twice in a week-long period for at least three months and does not lead to destruction of property or physical injury (Criterion A1).
- Three outbursts that involve injury or destruction within a year-long period (Criterion A2).
- Aggressive behavior is grossly disproportionate to the magnitude of the psychosocial stressors (Criterion B).
- The outbursts are not premeditated and serve no premeditated purpose (Criterion C).
- The outbursts cause distress or impairment of functioning, or lead to financial or legal consequences (Criterion D).
- The individual must be at least six years old (Criterion E).
- The recurrent outbursts cannot be explained by another mental disorder and are not the result of another medical disorder or substance use (Criterion F).

(American Psychiatric Association, 2013, pp. 466)

The symptoms cannot be better accounted for by another mental disorder, or by a medical condition, including a reaction to a medication or other psychotropic substance. *DSM-5* now includes two new specifiers for different subtypes of intermittent explosive episodes. One criterion includes behaviors that are lower intensity, but higher frequency, occurring on average twice weekly for three months. Behaviors in this category are not necessarily injurious or destructive and may include "temper tantrums, tirades, verbal arguments/fights, or assault without damage" (American Psychiatric Association, 2013, p. 467). The other criterion captures more intense and severe episodes that occur at a lower frequency, with the guideline of three times within a 12-month period. These behaviors are more assaultive and destructive and could include ". . . destroying an object without regard to value, assaulting an animal or individual" (American Psychiatric Association, 2013, p. 467).

The frequency of angry outbursts is high in even typical teenagers. A 2012 study of adolescent comorbidity in the United States found that nearly two-thirds of adolescents (63.3%) reported lifetime anger attacks that involved destroying property, threatening violence, or engaging in violence. Of these, 7.8% met criteria according to the *DSM-IV* or International Classification of Diseases (ICD) (World Health Organization) for a lifetime diagnosis of intermittent explosive disorder. The same study found that this group who met criteria had a mean onset of 12 years of age, and met a more persistent, 12-month criterion for the disorder. About 63.9% of the lifetime cases met criteria for other mental health diagnoses, including substance-use disorders. The authors noted that despite the fact that more than one-third (37.8%) of adolescents in the group had reported receiving treatment for emotional problems in the year before the interview, only 6.5% of these respondents were treated specifically for problems with anger (McLaughlin et al., 2012). The *DSM-5* estimates the prevalence of intermittent explosive disorder to be 2.7% in the United States (American Psychiatric Association, 2013, p. 467).

Intermittent explosive disorder in the past did not include verbal aggression as a criterion and was more defined by episodes that did not fit into other diagnoses, and which could not be explained by biological or neurological factors. In its previous form, intermittent explosive disorder could sometimes serve as a provisional diagnosis when a child had engaged in destructive behaviors and more information needed to be gathered. In its current form, more information is needed to better clarify etiology (McLaughlin et al., 2012; Oliver et al., 2016). However, it is believed to be a highly debilitating disorder in those who meet diagnostic criteria as it impacts one's ability to access education, a career, and meaningful relationships. Children who engage in what appear to be unpredictable and destructive episodes like the ones described in the diagnosis sometimes describe "blacking out" during the episode and they struggle to recall what occurred or what led up to the episode, which can make it difficult to engage in identifying triggers in therapy.

1.4   Pyromania

Pyromania refers to the deliberate and purposeful setting of fires and is included in the Disruptive Behavior Disorders section of the *DSM-5*. It includes "tension or affective arousal before the act" and "fascination with, interest in, curiosity about, or attraction to fire and its situational contexts (e.g., paraphernalia, uses, consequences)" (American Psychiatric Association, 2013, p. 476). An additional criterion is that the fire setting does not occur in the context of conduct disorder, a manic episode, or another disorder. This makes differential diagnosis a little more complex, since fire setting is also a symptom of conduct disorder. According to *DSM-5*, the lifetime prevalence of pyromania is not known. The prevalence of fire setting as a behavior was reported as 1.13% in a population sample, but as a primary diagnosis, pyromania appears to be very rare, adding "Among a sample of persons reaching the criminal justice system with repeated fire setting, only 3.3% had symptoms that met full criteria for pyromania" (American Psychiatric Association, 2013, p. 477). It is useful to remember that setting a fire as a means of protest or for monetary gain (as might happen with arson that was committed in hopes of accessing insurance money) is an exclusionary criterion for a diagnosis of pyromania. The exclusions also include setting a fire to conceal a crime, as an act of vengeance, in response to a hallucination or delusion or as a result of impaired judgment that might accompany an intellectual disability or intoxication (American Psychiatric Association, 2013, p. 476). This disorder generally occurs more in adults than in children.

1.5   Kleptomania

Kleptomania refers to repeated incidents of theft that are committed out of a compulsion or lack of impulse control, and not for monetary or other gain. In order to meet criteria for a diagnosis of kleptomania, the theft cannot be best explained as a symptom of conduct disorder, a manic episode, or antisocial personality disorder and cannot occur as a result of a hallucination, delusion, or as an act of revenge or anger against someone. The theft typically produces a release of tension or a sense of pleasure, relief, or gratification afterward. Interestingly, while most of the other disruptive behavior disorders are thought to be more prevalent in boys and men, kleptomania is estimated to occur among females at three times the rate it occurs in males. It is thought to occur in about 4% to 24% of all people who are arrested for shoplifting, although its prevalence in the general population is thought to only be 0.3% to 0.6% (American Psychiatric Association, 2013).

1.6   Antisocial Personality Disorder

Antisocial personality disorder, like all personality disorders, is considered to be a stable set of personality characteristics that develop over time. Unlike other disorders of behavior or emotion that may have a specific onset and then remission or recovery, personality disorders are thought to be more lasting because symptoms have now become part of a person's enduring repertoire of behavioral patterns, mindsets, and emotional coping strategies. Despite this, personality disorders do respond to treatment. In the last several years, Dialectical Behavior Therapy (DBT) has been found especially helpful for people diagnosed with Borderline Personality Disorder as well as those who struggle with substance abuse and other risk-taking behaviors. In the current *DSM*, antisocial personality disorder has also been cross-listed in the Disruptive Behavior Disorders category. Given that youth are still in the process of emotional and cognitive development well into and beyond their adolescent years (and even in their 20s according to newer neurological research), a personality disorder should never be diagnosed in an adolescent. The minimum age of diagnosis in the *DSM-5* for antisocial personality disorder is 18 years. The *DSM-5* also states that the criteria for the disorder have to have been met since age 15, and so three years of a pervasive pattern of disregard of the rights of others must be demonstrated to meet criteria for the diagnosis in an 18 year old. Despite these instructions, a clinician should consider the cognitive development and emotional maturity of the individual even if they are over 18 years before diagnosing a personality disorder, as they may not be equivalent to the individual's chronological age. Antisocial personality disorder carries with it a stigma and should not be diagnosed unless one feels fairly confident that this is the most accurate lens through which to view an individual's adjustment difficulties and behaviors. The *DSM* addresses social determinants of the disorder, cautioning the clinician:

> Antisocial personality disorder appears to be associated with low socioeconomic status and urban settings. Concerns have been raised that the diagnosis at times may be misapplied to individuals in settings in which seemingly antisocial behavior may be part of a protective survival strategy. In assessing antisocial traits, it is helpful for the clinician to consider the social and economic context in which the behaviors occur. (American Psychiatric Associationa, 2013, p. 662).

The prevalence of antisocial personality disorder is estimated to be between 0.2% and 3.3%, with the highest prevalence being found in men whose behaviors fall into the most severe on the continuum, and who are found in forensic settings such as prisons or substance abuse settings (American Psychiatric Association, 2013a). Prior to the publication of the most recent *DSM*, antisocial personality disorder was only listed under the "Personality Disorders" section of the *DSM*. In the newest version, it is listed in both the Personality Disorders as well as in the Disruptive Behavior Disorders sections.

CHAPTER 2

Conceptualization

2.1 Etiology: Genetic and Environmental Theories, Other Models

As is the case for almost all psychiatric diagnoses, both genetic and environmental factors have been identified as possible underlying causes of Disruptive Behavior Disorders. It can be challenging to identify the degree to which a condition is heritable because a person's biological parents very often create a large proportion of the environment in which the person is raised and thus, may be modeling behavioral dyscontrol. However, twin and adoption studies have shown that there appears to be an independent genetic influence on conduct disorder and other disruptive behavioral disorders (Cadoret, Yates, Ed, Woodworth, & Stewart, 1995; Rhee & Waldman, 2002) beyond a shared environmental influence. Similar results have been obtained for both males and females. Research has further demonstrated that there appears to be a high heritability factor for externalizing disorders generally (Hicks, Krueger, Iacono, McGue, & Patrick, 2004), meaning that children whose parents have any type of externalizing disorder are at increased risk for the development of any other type of externalizing disorder. Thus, it may be that the vulnerability for a lack of behavioral control is genetically inherited.

Conduct disorder and other disorders marked primarily by behavioral dysregulation have been conceptualized by some as a problem of neurology. There is a body of literature that shows that differences exist in brain structure and functioning in youth with conduct disorder compared to controls, particularly among youth who demonstrate conduct problems early in life (Moffitt, 2003). Not surprisingly, areas of the brain that seem to differ in structure or functioning among youth with persistent conduct problems include areas involved in functions such as emotion regulation or expression, decision making, and motivation. Many researchers, such as Sterzer, Stadler, Poustaka, and Kleinschmidt (2007) and Kruesi, Casanova, Mannheim, and Johnson-Bilder (2004), have found a lower volume of gray matter in the brain among youth with persistent conduct problems compared to control youth, and in one study, even compared to youth exclusively diagnosed with attention deficit hyperactivity disorder (ADHD) (Stevens & Haney-Caron, 2012). A recent study found that youth exhibiting callous–unemotional traits had particularly reduced gray matter volume even compared to youth diagnosed with conduct disorder, who are low on callous–unemotional traits (Sebastian et al., 2016), leading to speculation that brain differences among those with conduct problems might be specifically related to callous personality traits. Gray matter is present in regions of the brain involved in sensory processing and interpretation, decision making, cognitive flexibility, and self-control. Some of the specific areas of the brain that have frequently been found to be different in structure and/or function among youth with conduct disorder compared to controls are:

- The amygdala, which plays a key role in emotion, particularly fear and anger, emotional learning and behavior, and motivation.
- The insular cortex, or insula, which is believed to play a role in social emotions such as empathy, compassion, guilt, and remorse, in part by providing an emotional context for physiological experiences. The insula also plays a role in pain anticipation and response, and recognizing bodily desires for food, drugs, and sex.
- The anterior cingulate cortex, which is involved in decision making, impulse control, reward anticipation and emotion.
- Areas of the prefrontal cortex that are believed to play a role in decision making, including areas of the prefrontal cortex that may utilize information about emotions and rewards to make decisions.

Fairchild and colleagues (2013), noting that many studies regarding the neurological correlates of conduct disorder are conducted with males, have shown a similar pattern of neurological differences among females with conduct disorder compared to controls. Blair (2013) published a neurobiological model of conduct disorder that emphasizes the role of the amygdala. Blair noted that underactivation of the amygdala, leading to reduced empathy, is more likely to occur in those with callous–unemotional traits, whereas overactivation of the amygdala, leading to increased threat sensitivity and reactive aggression, is more likely to occur in those with a history of trauma. Particularly noteworthy, Finger and colleagues (2011) have shown underactivity in pathways in the brain that play a role in sensitivity to reinforcement, which may explain why youth with clinically significant behavior problems are less responsive than others to positive and negative consequences intended to modify their behavior, a treatment challenge familiar to many clinicians and others who work with these youth.

Many research studies examining the neurological correlates of conduct disorder endeavor to match subjects with conduct to disorder to controls on factors such as age and IQ to minimize potential confounds. However, it is important to recognize that the relationship between neurological functioning and psychopathology, including chronic conduct problems and other disruptive disorders, is complex and unlikely to be linear. For instance, many of the neurological differences that have been detected among those with chronic conduct problems may develop as a result of exposure to other known risk factors for conduct disorder, such as parents who exhibit conduct problems, poverty, deprivation, and trauma. However, youth who develop conduct problems may be more inclined to become stuck in or to seek out future environments and experiences that replicate those that contributed to early changes in neurological functioning. For instance, consider a youth who experienced ongoing violence in the home and later began demonstrating severe conduct problems. That youth's neurological functioning may have been impacted by his early traumatic experiences at home and possibly contributed to the development of conduct problems; however, as a result of his ongoing conduct problems, that youth later became involved in activities, such as robbery and drug dealing, that eventually exposed him to other traumas, such as his friends being shot or killed in his presence, and these traumas may further impact the functioning of the brain.

2.2   Disruptive Behavior Disorders and Controversy

There has long been debate and controversy over the best way to treat children with "acting out" or defiant behaviors, including whether or not these disorders should even be included in the *Diagnostic and Statistical Manual of Mental Disorders* (*DSM*). The most recent diagnostic description of oppositional defiant disorder (ODD) in the *DSM* cautions the reader to consider the role of culture, gender, and developmental level when trying to distinguish between psychopathology versus what may be in the realm of typical behavior for a given child. Similarly, the most recent *DSM* cautions readers to consider the environmental demands of a child or adolescent who may display symptoms of aggression, and consider whether or not those behaviors could be adaptive, or "survival skills" for a given setting. The newest edition of the *DSM* recognizes that these behaviors may serve an adaptive purpose and cautions against misapplying the label to individuals in settings where ". . . patterns of disruptive behavior are viewed as near-normative (e.g., in very threatening, high crime areas of war zones)" (American Psychiatric Association, 2013, p. 474). In his recent book, *Talking to Killers* (2015), psychologist and noted expert witness James Garbarino discusses the significant role of psychosocial stressors, particularly child abuse and exposure to violence, in the lives of young men and women who go on to commit murder. He discusses the notion of war zones in U.S. cities and how youth in these communities are affected. While in some communities, it is estimated that about 1% of residents will witness a murder in their lifetime, in more high-crime communities, that figure is as high as 43%. Similarly, the range of how many people can be expected to witness a stabbing spans from 9% to 55%, and the range of how many people might be expected to witness a shooting in their lifetime spans from 4% to 70% (Buka, Stichik, Birdthistle, & Earls, 2001, as cited in Garbarino, 2015). For the youth who live in communities where witnessing violence is on the higher end of this range, Garbarino (2015) writes "It is little wonder that brains develop capacities for 'overdeveloped threat detection' when threat is such an important part of the fabric of life" (p. 87). With the backdrop of violence and loss and the adaptive development of an increased sense of hypervigilance, the stage is set for a youth to respond aggressively to a perceived threat. Garbarino (2015) writes:

> Once immersed in this war zone mentality, youths act tough to ward off attacks from others (and to enhance their status with peers). The adolescent toward whom such gestures are directed is already hypervigilant, perceives even more threat than may be intended by the first youth, and thus responds aggressively (often with the hope of causing the other adolescent to back down). The first youth perceives the threat and responds with increased aggression. The cycle continues, and the war zone mentality flourishes. (p. 88)

A 2015 meta-analysis (Piotrowska, Stride, Croft, & Rowe, 2015) of socioeconomic status and antisocial behavior among children and adolescents looked at 133 studies that looked at these variables. They did find that consistent with prior research, being of low socioeconomic status is a significant risk factor for antisocial behavior in children and adolescents, although it varied by subtype of behavior. The link between poverty and ineffective or problematic parenting has been examined before.

The role of poverty also warrants further investigation into the underlying dynamics, and possibly a reframing of what is effective and ineffective for a given environmental demand. Children in high poverty and high stress situations, such as those with low family support or nurturance, are more at risk for developing behavior problems. In areas of high poverty, parents often face stressors that are more numerous and more pervasive, such as having to work multiple jobs and having to be more vigilant about their children's whereabouts if they live in a high-crime area. In high-poverty areas, after-school programs and safe, structured recreational outlets for youth are less available than they are in areas with overall higher socioeconomic status. Poverty and being socioeconomically disadvantaged in the United States are associated with a host of stressors that can lead to inadequate supervision due to multiple work responsibilities and less access to external supports, such as high-quality child care or adequately resourced schools. Poverty and its accompanying stressors also contribute to the cycle of coercive parenting, which is not only ineffective for managing childhood behavior problems but can contribute to their development.

Communities that are predominantly poor and under-resourced tend to be chaotic and dangerous, which can lead to the necessity of more controlled parenting, which in turn can hamper the development of self-regulation. Because of this and other demands on time and resources for parents living in poverty, harsh discipline and physical punishment have been found to be more prevalent. In turn, when children are more impulsive and tend to lose their temper more easily, parenting becomes more difficult and stressful, and parents can then be pushed to their limits patience-wise; middle and upper class parents also can reach this point but in poorer households there are fewer opportunities for parents to take a break or manage their own stress, and there may be less predictability and stability overall, which contributes to the cycle of overly punitive and coercive parenting.

In his most recent book on adolescence, noted adolescence expert Laurence Steinberg discussed the implications of newer research on the adolescent brain. The adolescent brain is notably less mature than the adult brain, which is reflected in increased impulsivity, less developed self-regulation, and poorer judgment. Neurological research has shown that the brain continues to mature past the age of 18 and into young adulthood. Concurrently, puberty has been moving steadily downward. In 2010, boys entered puberty a full two years earlier on average than they had in the 1970s. For girls, the average age of menarche, or first menstruation, is now 12, which means that many girls may be starting the beginning of puberty (marked by the development of breasts) as early as nine years old. At the same time, another marker of adulthood, the average age of marriage, has increased for both men and women by nearly a year per decade since 1950, ostensibly lengthening the period of adolescence in our society (Steinberg, 2014).

Children coming from impoverished backgrounds are more likely to enter puberty early. Multiple factors that may act upon the endocrine system to induce earlier onset of puberty can be present in all households, but there tends to be a higher probability that multiple factors are present in poorer households, including exposure to ongoing stress, higher incidence of childhood obesity, higher incidence of low birth weight for babies, and for girls whose biological father is not in the home, the exposure to pheromones of nonbiologically related males in the household may also induce early puberty (James, Ellis, Schlomer, & Garber, 2012; Steinberg, 2014).

Steinberg (2014) makes the case that this lengthened period of adolescence especially disadvantages children from poor families who may be less well-equipped to manage the challenges of early pubertal development. Because youth from impoverished households experience puberty at an earlier age, they may be more in need of external controls and supervision at a time when their hormones are acting upon their limbic system and increasing their reward-seeking behavior while their brains are still very malleable and plastic. The role of family supervision in managing adolescent difficulty with self-regulation and reckless and impulsive, reward-seeking behavior is an essential one. When it comes to the multiple evidence-based associations between adolescent risk behaviors (including delinquency as well as risks to oneself, like early substance use), parenting, and socioeconomic status, Steinberg notes:

> The bottom line is that children from wealthier families enter adolescence at a psychological advantage, and opportunities to further build the capacity for self-control are more plentiful for them. They enter secondary education with stronger self-regulation skills to begin with, having been raised in homes in which parents have stressed this trait. They're more likely to have parents and schools that can develop it further. Once they graduate high school, affluent adolescents are therefore more likely to have the psychological wherewithal and the financial resources to continue to continue their education. And because higher education itself contributes to prefrontal development, self-regulation begets more self-regulation. Young people from poorer families are more likely to enter into environments where opportunities for novelty and stimulation are lacking. The fact that poor children are less likely to receive environmental stimulation when they are young has received a great deal of attention. The fact that this deprivation continues well into adolescence, when the brain is also very plastic, is something that warrants more attention than it receives. (Steinberg, 2014, p. 176)

In some cases, addressing poverty may be the most effective intervention. A 2003 longitudinal study looked at the child psychiatric problems in a rural community sample comprised of 1,420 Native American and non-Native American, predominantly white, children who lived near one another. The groups had been divided into those who were persistently poor, those who had been poor but now were not, and those who had never been poor. Initially, higher levels of child psychopathology were found in the children who were both persistently poor and those who had been poor in their lifetime than in those children who had never been poor. During the eight years that the study was conducted, a casino was opened on the Native American reservation on which many of the Native American study participants lived, which resulted in annual income supplements to those participants. After the casino opened, incomes increased such that a proportion of the study participants moved from being persistently poor to not poor. When this occurred, their levels of psychopathology decreased to the same levels as those of the children in the "never-poor" group specifically around conduct disorder and ODD; levels of depression and anxiety remained unchanged. The same held true for the non-Native American children whose families also moved out of poverty during this period (Costello, Compton, Keeler, & Angold, 2003). The authors noted that in the never-poor sample, an increased income did not affect the level of psychopathology. They note that this naturally occurring experiment would lend support to looking at poverty as a causal factor for childhood conduct problems. One of the primary stressors that the increased income seemed to alleviate was what was defined as "lax supervision" or not always knowing the whereabouts of one's children. This decreased for those whose income increased, likely due to not needing to work as many hours or as many jobs, and so this may be an important component in looking at why and how the behavior problems improved.

2.3   Child Psychopathy

Is ODD a precursor to either conduct disorder or even to a trajectory of adult antisocial personality? More recent research has found more instability in callous–unemotional traits in youth over time, and suggests that these may more accurately demonstrate difficulties in adjustment at a given time in development, rather than a lifelong diagnosis. With proper and timely treatment, externalizing symptoms even in children with callous and unemotional traits can be ameliorated and treated (Muratori et al., 2016).

In his 2016 review of literature on conduct disorder, Frick looks at various developmental pathways to conduct disorder. The predominant thinking on conduct disorder, and specifically, children and teens with callous–unemotional traits, was that these were a likely precursor to later antisocial behavior and somewhat resistant to treatment. A 2003 meta-analysis of various studies found that youth with conduct disorder were 17 times more likely than youth without conduct disorder to develop antisocial personality disorder (Burke, Loeber, & Lahey, 2003). However, this is less clear cut than it might appear. Newer research has found that it may not simply be whether or not a youth is diagnosed with conduct disorder that can increase the likelihood of whether or not that youth later develops lifelong antisocial traits, but more complex factors and different ways of calculating various risk and protective factors that mediate the effects of the diagnosis. The research that has looked at these other factors has found associations between the number and types of symptoms of conduct disorder, as well as the contribution of substance-use problems, which tend to put youth in the company of more troubled peers and also create a financial strain. Still other research has looked at the contribution of comorbid diagnoses of ADHD and ODD to later development of antisocial behaviors. There have also been associations of antisocial behavior with internalizing disorders, namely depression. Interestingly, anxiety problems may serve a more protective function for these youth in preventing later antisocial behaviors, as the anxiety increases inhibitory responses and is incongruent with callousness (Washburn et al., 2007).

A 2007 study of youth in a juvenile detention facility found that covert rather than overt antisocial behavior seemed to be one of the risk factors that was associated with development of more antisocial traits after a three-year follow up (Washburn et al., 2007) as did a disorder of alcohol use, which was hypothesized to further lower inhibitions and possibly lead to more explosive behavior. This study acknowledges that African American males are overrepresented in juvenile detention, as are youth whose families are considered to be living in poverty. Poverty and socioeconomic status also have strong associations with conduct problems in youth (Costello, Compton, Keeler, & Angold, 2003; Steinberg, 2014; Steiner & Remsing, 2007) and so these may have also been predisposing factors in the study.

2.4 Biological and Environmental Causes

When the creators of the first DSM were first convened, they one day envisioned a world where neurobiology and genetic models would advance such that there might be genetic or biological markers for most mental illnesses, which in turn would elevate the field of psychiatric diagnosis and leave less room for subjectivity or error. While advances in the fields of genetics and neurobiology have advanced significantly since the creation of the first edition of the *DSM* in 1952, psychiatric diagnosis remains socially constructed to greater and lesser degrees. However, this may also reflect a greater understanding of the interplay between "nature" and "nurture." The commonly used stress-diathesis model posits that mental illnesses are caused by an underlying genetic vulnerability, environmental factors, and protective factors (Linehan, 1993). For a psychiatric condition such as schizophrenia, this model posits that an individual has to have an underlying biological disposition for the disorder, which can then be triggered or exacerbated by social, biological, and psychological stressors. In some cases, the stress to the body caused by puberty can trigger a condition.

Dr. Marsha Linehan, the creator of Dialectical Behavior Therapy, describes the "dialectical" or "transactional" models as alternatives to the more traditional interaction models, such as the stress-diathesis model:

> In contrast a dialectical or transactional model assumes that individual functioning and environmental conditions are mutually and continuously interactive, reciprocal, and interdependent. Within social learning theory, this is the principle of 'reciprocal determinism': The environment and the individual adapt to and influence each other. Although the individual is surely affected by the environment, the environment is also affected by the individual. (Linehan, 1993, p. 39)

This sentiment is echoed in the transactional model of conduct disorder and other childhood mental health diagnoses, which proposes that there is an interplay of situational and temperamental factors that interact with each other (Dodge & Pettit, 2003; Frick, 2016; "Practice Parameter," 2007). Underlying biological or temperamental factors can interact with environmental or situational factors in a way that affects both. This can hold true for not only predisposing or risk factors, but also for protective factors that can ameliorate risk factors and decrease underlying vulnerabilities. Enrollment in an early childhood program, such as "Headstart," and participation in a program that works with both children and parents, such as "The Incredible Years," are examples. Working to improve parenting strategies and management of parental stress while addressing child behavior problems in effective and manageable ways can dramatically alter the trajectory of a child even when there may be underlying biological dispositions that would place that child at increased risk.

The difference between children with frequent conduct problems, who display an average level of callous-unemotional traits, and their peers with higher levels of callous-unemotional traits is notable. In studies of responses to affective stimuli, the children with average levels of callous–unemotional traits displayed higher reactivity to upsetting emotional stimuli. They also respond to punishment and consequences. By contrast, their peers with a high level of callous-unemotional traits showed significantly lower reactivity to emotional stimuli and are far less sensitive to punishment or fearful of consequences (Frick, 2016). As one might imagine, the temperament of the child with callous-unemotional traits might pose specific challenges to parenting in a way that is warm and which promotes consistent rules and boundaries. As a result, the type of harsh, coercive, and inconsistent parenting that is associated with conduct disorder may be reinforced in what can become a vicious cycle. Part of breaking this cycle is training caregivers to respond in a way that is less emotionally reactive and more proactive in order to begin to change the dynamic.

James Garbarino (2015) discusses the role of untreated trauma and violence in his book, *Listening to Killers: Lessons Learned From My 20 Years as a Psychological Expert Witness in Murder Cases*. Garbarino shares stories of his interviews and his attempts to develop a comprehensive understanding of people convicted of murder. Many of these people grew up in troubled households, or what Garbarino refers to as war zones, and nearly all experienced untreated trauma, often multiple traumas and severely problematic caregiving. Garbarino discusses the issue of poor decision making in these individuals as a false or faulty premise based on the assumptions that free will and informed consent are present, which they are not. In his discussion on the paucity of choices and "free will," Garbarino writes:

> The larger point is that choices are always made in a context. Violent youths have typically grown up in contexts where trauma—untreated trauma—is typically the rule rather than the exception. This untreated trauma often makes them 'dangerous' in the sense that they are driven by unconscious motivations that predispose them to bad choices. From their perspective, the range of options realistically available to them is so narrow that there is no "good choice," at least in the way mainstream society would classify it. The options appear to be especially narrow for males who carry a profound sadness—and accompanying rage—in a culture that teaches boys that 'it is better to be mad than to be sad.' Sometimes this leads to horrific choices. (Garbarino, 2015, p. 37)

CHAPTER 3

Evaluation and Assessment

3.1 Differential Diagnosis and Best Practice in Assessment: The Importance of a Good History and Clinical Interview

A good assessment always hinges upon a detailed and thorough clinical interview. While the clinical interview should not be the only part of an evaluation, it is an essential part of both the diagnosis and assessment process. Structured, norm-referenced, standardized interviews such as the Kiddie SADS Present and Lifetime Version (K-SADS-PL, Matuschek et al., 2016) or the Diagnostic Interview Schedule for Children Predictive Scales (DISC, Wiesner, Windle, Kanouse, Elliott, & Schuster, 2015) have the benefits of standardization, but it is critical, as with all structured interviews, that the clinician or researcher administering the interview have a strong understanding of context and developmental appropriateness. It is also important to look at the validity of any scale for the population with which it is being used. This becomes especially important when working with a diverse population, (i.e., children of color, second-language learners, or children with developmental disabilities). One should look at the population on which the scale was normed to better understand its validity for a given client, especially if a client is from an ethnic, cultural, or racial minority population.

An unstructured clinical interview allows for more freedom in the directions of questions, but should only be conducted by an experienced evaluator who has a good background in typical childhood development. It is crucial that an evaluator utilizing an unstructured interview format understands which responses require additional queries or follow-up information. The evaluator must also understand other considerations related to development and culture.

Trying to evaluate whether or not a child is experiencing auditory or visual hallucinations is one such example where clinician experience and training is crucial. While past research has shown that typically young children can distinguish fantasy from reality by ages three or four (Gilpin, Brown, & Pierucci, 2015), it is age appropriate for children to engage in magical thinking and fantasy even as late as ages eight or nine (Woolley, 1997); children who experience adversity may have an even stronger tendency to utilize fantasy as a coping style. For a typically developing child who is under the age of nine or ten, a report of hearing voices or seeing a ghost may represent a rich fantasy life, an attempt to cope with stress, or, especially in the case of children aged five and younger under, an age-appropriate stage of cognitive development (Berkowski & MacDonald, 2014; Woolley, 1997). It is not uncommon for children to have "imaginary friends" from ages three to eight, and some may persist until age ten (Woolley, 1997).

Other times young children who have been exposed to movies or television shows with violent or scary content retell what they have seen without a clear indication to the listener that this is from the movie. When this occurs in a young child, it may not suggest that the child is experiencing hallucinations, but that they were exposed to inappropriate content that has been causing them distress, and this is certainly data that can help inform case conceptualization. There are also families who are religiously or spiritually affiliated with a faith emphasizing "spirits" that may be conceptualized as interacting with the living. When conducting interviews with people who adhere to these cultural or faith traditions, it is neither atypical nor an indicator of child psychopathology for a child to report seeing or hearing a deceased relative or other acquaintance. An interview with a caregiver can help clarify whether the child's statements are consistent with cultural norms within the family or home setting.

Follow-up questioning and knowing when to query for more details is a key component of either type of interview. An example of this can occur with the behavior of killing or hurting an animal. Taken on its own, animal cruelty, broadly defined, was long considered to be one of the traits of the now mostly debunked "Sociopathic Triad," along with bedwetting and fire setting. Even without the presence of other symptoms, animal cruelty is still a behavior of great concern and thought to be predictive of possible future antisocial behavior (Tallichet & Hensley, 2004). However, the details around why and how an animal got injured or killed by a child make a significant difference in understanding the motivation behind the act. Some children injure animals accidentally without having any malicious intentions or even impulse control difficulties; they simply do not yet understand certain truths about animals and their care (i.e., wanting to give a kitten a "bath" in a bucket) and may not have been supervised sufficiently during the event. Other children still do not have malicious intent but have a difficult time managing their impulses (i.e., the child who pushes or throws a small pet without thinking about the consequences). Yet other children do have intent to harm an animal and engage in this behavior knowing exactly what will occur (i.e., the child who pours bleach into a fish tank and understands that the fish will die as a result). Regardless of the motivation and function of the behavior, supervision and psycho education of a child who harms an animal is essential; in some cases, it may be appropriate to recommend that a child live in a home with no pets to ensure safety, but it is crucial to understand why a child harmed an animal before making any treatment recommendations. It is especially important to consider the details of the animal cruelty before considering it to be a "callous" trait simply on its own.

3.2   Assessment of Children with Global Impairment/Developmental Concerns

For children who may be on the Autism Spectrum, or who may be cognitively impaired, an interview needs to be conducted keeping in mind that these children may have underdeveloped social skills and emotional problem solving more typical of a much younger child, despite their chronological age. In the case of high functioning youth with an autism spectrum disorder (ASD), it is important to remember that in some cases the impairment is primarily one of social skills and emotional engagement, and so even in cases where a child has average to above average cognitive and academic functioning, their motivations and behaviors in social situations may not be commensurate with these other abilities. A recent study found that 60% of one population of adolescent male sex offenders, who were being treated in a residential facility, met criteria for ASD (Sutton et al., 2013). Diagnosis of ASD in a population, such as this one, is extremely important so as to make sure that youth with ASD get appropriate treatment. It is also important that youth with ASD are grouped appropriately so as to reduce any vulnerability that may increase when they are in groups or other treatment settings with neurotypical youth with antisocial behaviors, who may target them for harassment.

A good records review can help alert an evaluator to any potential cognitive or emotional delays for a client. Conversely, it should never be assumed that an individual with a previous diagnosis of an ASD or a history of pervasive developmental delay will necessarily be cognitively below his or her chronological age; so in preparing for an evaluation of such a client, one must be prepared for a few possible lines of questioning or types of scales for different age ranges.

A client who is unable to read at the appropriate level should never be left on his or her own to complete a self-report form and should obtain assistance in the reading and responding; the same may be true for caregivers who have difficulty reading or who are not native speakers of the language of the assessment. Many checklists come in translated forms and culturally competent practice should include translated report forms as appropriate to the needs of the clientele.

In trying to assess a child's cognitive abilities, one can generally assume that a cognitive assessment administered within two years should still be valid, barring any major injury or other significant event that may affect cognition (i.e., a neurological insult). However, it is important to keep in mind that when considering a diagnosis of intellectual disability, a child must not only demonstrate a valid IQ score under 70, but must also demonstrate significant impairment in one or more life skills, such as communication or self-care. The new *DSM-5* diagnostic criteria for intellectual disability include assessing an individual's functioning in the areas of conceptual, practical, and social skills. These can be measured with the use of adaptive skills scales, such as the Vineland and Adaptive Behavior Assessment System, second edition (ABAS-2) (Papazoglou, Jacobson, McCabe, Kaufmann, & Zabel, 2014).

For both children with and without developmental delay, as well as for younger children, utilizing the procedures that are broadly under the umbrella of Functional Analyses (Watson, Gresham, & Skinner, 2001) can be an excellent, non-norm referenced way to get more information about the function of problematic behaviors. These procedures, which include a functional behavior analysis (FBA), can be helpful to identify the antecedents and environmental factors that can trigger a behavior, as well as the consequences and factors that serve to maintain that behavior. Functional assessment procedures can include direct observation or direct experimental intervention. It can also involve indirect procedures such as the use of interviews and rating scales completed by caregivers, teachers, residential or other therapeutic support staff, and others who have frequent contact with the child in a relevant setting. FBA is often used to determine if a child is acting aggressively due to a need to avoid a task, to gain attention, as a means of communicating a need, or another reason that may only become apparent when a third party is observing and collecting data.

Previously, FBAs were primarily used in the context of work with children with developmental delays or with intellectual disabilities, but they have increasingly been used to assist with other problem behaviors with more varied students. In schools, an FBA is necessary to develop a Behavior Intervention Plan when a student has engaged in behavior that interferes with their learning. Under the last reauthorization of the federal mandate for special education in 2004, the Individuals with Disabilities in Education Act (IDEA) strengthened the language that specifically speaks to the use of a Functional Behavior Analyses and Behavior Intervention Plans to address student behavior problems, especially as they relate to disciplinary problems. Each state differs in their specific guidelines around the use of these procedures and some states encourage or require their use more strongly than does the federal law, while some states do not encourage or require it as strongly as does IDEA, and so in a school setting, local guidelines must also be considered when considering the necessity of these procedures (Zirkel, 2011). While the law does not specify who is qualified to complete an FBA, it is incumbent upon a school to ensure that there are professionals who have been appropriately trained in conducting these. It may also reduce potential liability for a school district to ensure that FBAs are conducted by appropriate staff.

3.3   Test Batteries and Checklists

Generally, externalizing behaviors can be assessed through the use of a comprehensive child behavior checklist, such as the Achenbach scales. The most commonly used version of checklist for children is the Child Behavior Checklist (CBCL), which is normed for children aged 6 to 18 years. The checklist can be completed by a caregiver. A self-report scale, the Youth Self Report (YSR), is available for children aged 11 to 18 years, and there is also a Teacher Report Form (TRF), and a version of the CBCL for ages 1½ to 5 years, which also include a language inventory to assess for possible language delay. The CBCL includes indices for Externalizing and Internalizing behaviors, and also has a DSM scale which interprets scores as aligned with symptom clusters from the *DSM-5* (Rescorla et al., 2014).

Similarly, the Behavioral Assessment System for Children (BASC) can be used as a global assessment of child behavior and mental health symptoms (Reynolds & Kamphaus, 2015). The BASC, now in its third edition, measures behaviors along 14 indices which include Hyperactivity, Aggression, and Conduct Problems, along with Internalizing problems, such as Withdrawal and Anxiety, and Adaptive skills. It has also been updated to better align with *DSM-5* diagnostic criteria, but unlike the CBCL, does not have DSM specific scales.

There are also scales intended to measure externalizing or problematic behaviors more specifically. The Millon Adolescent Clinical Inventory (MACI) is designed to assess psychopathology in youth aged 13 to 19 years and has been intended for use in clinical settings (Millon & Davis, 1993). While it is among the shorter of the other scales developed by Millon and colleagues, it is 160 items and is written on a sixth-grade reading level. This length and reading level can make it difficult for children with any attention difficulties or reading difficulties to complete it accurately, and so any clinician wishing to use this measure should consider its appropriateness for a given client who may experience difficulty in either of these areas. To date, there is less research on psychopathy in children than there is for adults; however, this has been a growing area of research and clinical focus, and the added specifier of Limited Prosocial Emotion in the *DSM-5* seeks to describe some of these markers of potential child psychopathy. Gacono and Hughes (2004) recommend utilizing a checklist of psychopathy with adolescents and children when trying to organize clinical information and to help determine the most appropriate treatment. The Psychopathy Checklist: Youth Version (PCL: YV) (Hemphala & Hodgins, 2014) can be used for this purpose.

When administering scales for the purpose of diagnosis, it is important to keep in mind that behaviors must be present in multiple settings (i.e., to ensure that this is not a matter of a single individual such as a teacher or caregiver who is having a difficult time with a child or who is unfamiliar with what may be typical reactions to stressors). Ideally, more than one reporter's observations can be obtained, either through checklists or interviews, or both. The Achenbach has the TRF which can be given to teachers to complete. A records review should include school records as well as reports from caregivers and from the child themself.

3.4   Differential Diagnosis in DSM-5

With regard to differential diagnosis, the *DSM-5* notes a high level of comorbidity for conduct disorder and oppositional defiant disorder (ODD) and also notes that ODD is frequently a precursor to the later development of conduct disorder. Past editions of the *DSM* (4th ed., text rev., 2000; 4th ed., 1994) did not allow for the diagnosis of both conduct disorder and ODD in the same individual. The *DSM-IV* (American Psychiatric Association, 1994) and *DSM-IV-TR* (American Psychiatric Association, 2000) instructed that a diagnosis of ODD was not to be rendered if the individual met criteria for conduct disorder. However, the *DSM-5* notes that a persistent pattern of angry and irritable behavior is a marker for ODD, but not conduct disorder, and allows for the diagnosis of both disorders when criteria for both are met.

The *DSM-5* makes a distinction between conduct disorder and intermittent explosive disorder, noting that while aggressive behavior is associated with both disorders, aggression associated with conduct disorder is often "proactive and predatory" (American Psychiatric Association, 2013, p. 469), whereas the aggressive behavior associated with intermittent explosive disorder is typically highly impulsive in response to acute emotional provocation and is "not committed to achieve some tangible objective" (p. 475). While the *DSM-5* does not prohibit concurrently diagnosing conduct disorder and intermittent explosive disorder, it seems to urge caution, noting that both diagnoses should be given only when the type of impulsive aggressive outbursts associated with intermittent explosive disorder warrant independent clinical attention.

Two specific disorders of impulse control, pyromania and kleptomania, are listed in the *DSM-5* in the same section as conduct disorder. Pyromania involves a repeated pattern of intentionally setting fires, while kleptomania is marked by a pattern of stealing objects not needed for personal use or monetary value. Both fire setting and theft are behaviors that may occur in the context of conduct disorder and are included in the list of 15 possible indicators of conduct disorder. For both pyromania and kleptomania, the final diagnostic criteria notes that the disorder should not be diagnosed if the fire-setting behavior or stealing behavior, respectively, can be better explained by another disorder listed, one of which is conduct disorder. The *DSM-5* reiterates in the discussion of these diagnoses that conduct disorder is marked by a pattern of antisocial behavior, whereas both pyromania and kleptomania are marked by the singular disruptive behavior noted.

A relatively high proportion of adopted children display externalizing behavior problems. This has been documented in various ways and for various reasons since the 1960s (Simmel, Brooks, Garth, & Hinshaw, 2001). This American study which used norm-referenced assessments in a statewide sample of adopted children found that 21% of the children in their study met criteria for attention deficit hyperactivity disorder (ADHD) and 20% of the children they surveyed met criteria for ODD, with or without a comorbid diagnosis of ADHD (Simmel et al., 2001). This could have to do with the genetics of the child's biological family, the influence of the time spent in the child welfare system, which can expose children to abuse, neglect, and peer aggression, or the dynamics between an adoptive family and the child postadoption.

At the same time, there is a disturbing trend in overdiagnosis of this population with reactive attachment disorder (RAD) or developmental attachment disorder (DAD) (Chaffin et al., 2006; Woolgar & Baldock, 2015; Woolgar & Scott, 2014) in children whose difficulties may best be characterized by more common diagnoses such as ODD, Impulse

Control Disorder, or ADHD. In their 2015 article on best practice guidelines, Woolgar and Baldock (2015) advise, "Consistent with the practice parameters (Chaffin et al., 2006) assessments of looked after and adopted children should prioritize the identification of common disorders to open up evidence-based care pathways" (p. 1).

Children who are most accurately diagnosed with RAD or DAD, which is thought to be about 1% of the population ("Practice Parameter," 2005), can also demonstrate behaviors which are oppositional and defiant, and which sometimes appear to be callous and unemotional with caregivers and others, and so there can be overlap between these diagnoses.

One of the main criteria for RAD is a history of pathogenic care, which can include neglect or institutionalization at a young age. Pathogenic care as a stressor can also result in symptoms of post-traumatic stress disorder (PTSD). In *DSM-5*, one cluster of symptoms of PTSD is defined as "marked alterations in arousal and reactivity" (American Psychiatric Association, 2013). In order to be considered for the diagnosis, one has to meet at least two of the following symptoms from this cluster which include, "irritable behavior and angry outbursts (with little or no provocation) typically expressed as verbal or physical aggression toward people or objects" (p. 272), as well as hypervigilance, exaggerated startle response, and "reckless or self-destructive behavior" (p. 272). Clearly, there is overlap diagnostically between a disorder that is best conceived as being a disruptive behavior disorder and possible post-traumatic stress. To further complicate things, it is not unusual for children and adolescents and adults who are referred for aggression or other problematic externalizing behaviors to have a history of exposure to a significant stressor, or multiple stressors, in their past. A history of trauma and/or exposure to multiple or chronic stressors can even be a contributing cause for conduct disorder or more serious antisocial behaviors.

In a case like this, conducting a thorough clinical interview and gathering a good history, preferably from multiple informants, is especially critical to case conceptualization and diagnosis. If the externalizing symptoms were mostly or entirely not present before an identifiable trauma, and appeared to emerge afterward, then this would more clearly point toward PTSD. However, in cases where the trauma may take the form of multiple chronic stressors, which can include caregiver instability, housing instability, the drug abuse or mental illness of a primary caregiver, or exposure to violence or domestic abuse, the primary diagnosis may not be as clear. In a case such as this, a provisional diagnosis of a disruptive behavior disorder alongside either a provisional or more certain diagnosis of PTSD may be appropriate, with the recommendation that diagnosis be revisited after engagement in treatment.

3.5   Cultural Competence in Assessment

Cultural competence is an ethical imperative in assessment. Prior to administering either a structured or unstructured assessment, a clinician should ascertain as best possible whether or not the client being assessed, or in the case of a child, that client's caregivers, are fluent enough in spoken English or if they will benefit from an interpreter. The best practice in administering norm-referenced tests to speakers of another language would be to have the tests administered by a qualified professional who is also a speaker of that language. If that is not possible, then a translator should be sought. Fluency in written English is also important to ascertain for both second-language learners of English as well as for native speakers of English. A parent who has difficulty reading should not be given a written checklist such as the Behavior Assessment System for Children–Parent Checklist, which is written on a sixth-grade reading level, to complete on their own. Likewise, a native speaker of English who struggles in reading or with attention should not left on their own to complete (either on paper or online) a long written form that may require both fluency in reading and focused attention. Giving an adolescent with this profile (many of whom are referred for assessment based on impulsivity), a written checklist of over 400 items, such as is the case with the Minnesota Multiphasic Personality Assessment, Adolescent Version (MMPI-A), can result in an obviously invalid administration, such as was the case when a teenager returned a MMPI-A booklet with a beautifully designed vertically crisscrossing pattern across the page. Sometimes, a completed checklist may look valid but should not be considered as such if it cannot be guaranteed that the person completing it could read it fluently or give it their full attention throughout.

Aside from completion of written checklists, the role of culture in understanding the functioning of a family or child cannot be overstated. An element of this involves marginalization. In the United States, a given family can be marginalized due to poverty, education status, disability status, race, ethnicity, or immigrant status, as well as sexual orientation, gender identity, and ability status. When interviewing a family who may have previously experienced legitimate or perceived systemic discrimination or difficulty with power structures, it is important to keep in mind that their previous negative experiences may cause them to present as less open or even hostile during the assessment process. Diagnosing clinicians may be apt to label this "resistance" or "noncompliance;" however, this may not accurately reflect what has occurred.

The best way to understand the culture and previous experiences of a given family or child is to ask, listen nonjudgmentally, and then do follow-up research when appropriate. In one such case, a clinician one of the writers supervised described as "uncooperative" the mother of a child who appeared hostile during the process of coming to an evaluation with her daughter and her own mother. In interviewing this mother privately, it was discovered that she herself had experienced multiple significant traumas, which were exacerbated by being a poor African American woman during a time where both of these factors limited one's access to good health care or adequate housing. This parent had contracted a life-threatening disease as a result of one of these traumas, which left her feeling physically weak many days, as she did today. She explained that her mother, who had accompanied her to the evaluation, was very critical of her parenting and she felt resentful that her mother had minimized her own difficulties when she was a child following her own experiences of abuse. After understanding the lived experiences and concerns of this parent, we were not only better able to place her behavior at the evaluation in context, but were also better able to understand the larger environmental and historical context of the child's and family's difficulties, which helped to better inform treatment. For a parent or family who is already mistrustful of authority or of mental health services, adding derogatory subjective assessments such as "poor historian" or "resistant" can not only take away from a more accurate understanding of family dynamics, but can also serve to feed into the mistrust and disengagement a family may feel when reading the report.

For clients who may be transgender or gender variant, it sometimes may be the case that the name on their medical record is not the name that they choose when being addressed by others. A safe way to ensure that every client is being called by a name with which they are comfortable is to ask all clients, regardless of appearance, what they like to be called when one begins an evaluation or a therapeutic relationship. This may help with rapport building with all clients, especially with children who often have nicknames.

When considering the role of culture, broad understandings of history and various identity statuses are necessary; but ultimately, understanding the given culture of an individual, how their multiple identities or statuses intersect, and the meanings they have ascribed to the events in their life is essential. In an assessment context, this often means learning enough about your client prior to the evaluation to adequately prepare, while also keeping an open mind when the person is sitting in front of you about how their multiple identities interact with their lived experiences.

3.6   Risk Management: Balancing Compassion With Safety

An essential element of assessment when working with children and teens who engage in problematic behaviors against others is to assess risk while also considering that children and adolescents are quantitatively different entities than are adults. Newer research on the adolescent brain has identified that cognitive development and reasoning skills continue to develop beyond the legally defined upper limit of 18 years of age (Steinberg, 2014). The pioneer of much of this research, Dr. Laurence Steinberg, has been instrumental in also working with lawmakers to set more scientifically grounded punishments for youth who commit crimes, such as eliminating life without parole for juveniles. Steinberg describes the adolescent brain as fundamentally more immature than the adult brain when it comes to impulse control, self-regulation, and decision making, three factors which often play a role in the commission of crimes.

When this immature reasoning is paired with the significant influence of peers and some of the other hallmarks of adolescence, such as increased risk taking and a sense of invulnerability, disastrous things can occur.

Neuroscience has helped us to understand some of the vast differences in judgment between an adolescent or even a person in their early 20s and an adult. For this reason, risk assessments of children and adolescents should be revisited on a periodic basis and no long-term, permanent decisions should be made based on assessments done while one was a juvenile.

In the area of sexual offense assessment, a structured, norm-based measure, such as the J-SOAP-II (Prentky & Righthand, 2003), J-SORRAT-II (Epperson, Ralston, Fowers, & DeWitt, 2005), or ERASOR (Worling & Curwen, 2000), can help to give a picture of overall risk of reoffense with both dynamic and static factors for boys aged from 12 to 18 years. No risk assessment should be based only on these measures, but as part of a more comprehensive evaluation which involves obtaining history, ideally from caregivers and others. In recent years, protective factors, such as social support, have become more of a focus in community settings. The Good Life Model (Barnao, Ward, & Robertson, 2016), a framework which has at the center of it the person, has become an alternative model for supporting gains made in treatment of offenders with co-occurring mental health challenges. The model seeks to increase a client's access to things that increase their quality of life and work toward meeting their personal goals, such as the attainment of a satisfying job, while also balancing safety needs for the community. For those supporting juveniles in the community, there has always been a balance of providing the needed supervision while taking care not to make the juvenile a pariah or alienated from peers, which would then lower protective factors and increase the risk of re-offense.

3.7   Risk Assessment in Violent Youth

For youth who have demonstrated violent or antisocial behavior, the Structured Assessment of Violence Risk in Youth, or SAVRY (Borum, Bartel, & Forth, 2003), can be used along with a clinical interview to help determine risk of engaging in future violence. The SAVRY consists of one static scale and two dynamic scales, and also includes protective factors (Borum et al., 2003).

The PCL: YV (Forth, Kosson, & Hare, 2003) is designed to measure traits of psychopathy among juveniles aged 12 to 18 years. While traits of psychopathy and antisocial behavior have been used to predict sexual offense risk, these instruments are shown to have been weaker at prediction of sexual offense than the measures specifically designed for this purpose (Hempel, Buck, Cima, & van Marle, 2013).

When one is dealing with a potentially violent youth, supervision is of the utmost importance. Knowing the exact living situation of the youth, who sleeps where, whether or not supervision is being provided by a responsible adult, whether or not there are vulnerable children in the home, and access to weapons is essential. If a child has a history of cruelty toward animals, then they should not reside in a home with pets, or short of that and depending on the severity and motivation behind the incident, should not be left alone with pets.

While pyromania is generally diagnosed by a psychologist or psychiatrist, a fire safety assessment can also be done by specialists who can be found in either mental health settings, or in fire departments in some locations. For a child or adolescent who presents with any fire-setting concerns, a fire-setting evaluation can help determine the level of risk and best inform what safety and supervision precautions need to be followed in the child's home or treatment and school settings.

CHAPTER 4

Treatment

4.1 Identifying Best Practice

The practice of "zero tolerance" policies in schools, which began during the Reagan administration of the 1980s and picked up steam after the highly publicized school shootings in the 1990s, is now being questioned, and educators and mental health professionals are looking to more effective approaches (National Association of School Psychologists [NASP], 2001; Skiba, 2000). In recent years, there has been an effort by researchers, clinicians, and policy makers to try to not only identify programs that are supported by empirical research and work well across various populations of children and families, but also to disseminate those programs to those working in communities as easily and effectively as possible. To this end, there have been several federal or grant-funded initiatives to gather these interventions and then provide an easy way for providers and others to access them via the Internet. The "Blueprints for Healthy Youth Development" website (http://blueprintsprograms.com/) is one such initiative that is a project of the Center for the Study and Prevention of Violence at University of Colorado, Boulder, with funding from the Annie E. Casey Foundation. The website can be searched by outcome desired (i.e., a reduction in substance abuse, bullying prevention), and the demographics of the target population. On the site, over 1,400 programs have been reviewed for evidence of effectiveness, specificity of claims, readiness for dissemination, and quality of the evaluation efforts used through reviewing research done by scholars in the field, which is then reviewed by an advisory panel. Only 5% have been labeled as either "promising" or "model," with some programs being identified as "model plus" (retrieved from http://blueprintsprograms .com/about).

Other databases of effective programs to address behavior that can lead to delinquency and involvement in crime are managed by the Office of Juvenile Justice and Delinquency Prevention (www.ojjdp .gov/mpg) and the National Institute of Justice (www.crimesolutions .gov/). The Substance Abuse and Mental Health Services Administration (SAMHSA) maintains a similar database called the National Registry of Evidence-based Programs and Practices (NREPP) that contains 350 substance abuse and mental health interventions (www.nrepp.samhsa .gov), as does the Coalition for Evidence-based Policy (toptierevidence .org/), which is a nonprofit organization funded by the Laura and John Arnold Foundation.

Part of deciding what will be the most effective intervention for a given child or family struggling with conduct issues depends on determining the function of the behavior. Treatment cannot be "one size fits all" for children and teens who struggle with conduct and behavior problems. There are many treatments and treatment modalities that have evidence to support their effectiveness for behavior and conduct problems, some of which are federally mandated for school districts through the Individuals with Disabilities in Education Act (IDEA), most recently reauthorized in 2004.

4.2   Cognitive Behavioral Therapy

For many children who struggle in the family or other settings, cognitive behavioral therapy (CBT) can be of great benefit both individually or as a family treatment modality (Battagliese et al., 2015). CBT has a strong evidence base behind it. At its core, CBT helps clients identify their thoughts, feelings, and actions, and then examine them more closely, with the guiding principle that our thoughts, feelings, and actions are all connected and impact one another. By examining one's thoughts, one can often identify cognitions and beliefs that are inaccurate or dysfunctional in some way, and then modify them through a variety of means in order to then alter the frame through which one views events. Changing the framework or the thoughts around events then leads to a different emotional experience and, consequently, may then lead to behavior change. For example, a person who has an overly negative worldview or who may suffer from depression, may take the feedback of others as overly negative when it is not intended to be. These thoughts may then continue to reinforce the person's negative feelings about themself and their abilities. Helping the person to reframe how they interpret this feedback and working to ensure more accurate cognitions may then serve to change their feelings and views to a more accurate and less negative portrayal. CBT can also involve many other tools that work to target thoughts, feelings, and behaviors, including self-regulation, identification of feelings and thoughts, and effective coping with difficult emotions and relaxation exercises. CBT tends to be targeted and is geared toward a relatively short-term resolution of therapy, as opposed to a psychoanalytic or more general client-directed model that may require extended periods of time. There are many different manualized treatments and therapy models that are based on CBT principles, and the length, duration, and goals of these models vary depending on the target issue and target audience (i.e., children with anxiety, families of children with behavior problems, or children who engage in sexually problematic behaviors), but most CBT models of treatment involve homework and may involve some level of structure around sessions and agenda setting. The strong evidence base, effectiveness, relative efficiency, and measurable outcomes make CBT not only a good fit for clinical research but also a good fit for managed care systems and private insurance companies.

For a parent or family component, CBT programs may utilize behavior modification or behavior analytic theory and techniques. These may consist of teaching parents to reward positive prosocial behavior through reinforcement, to not react punitively to minor misbehavior and to use developmentally appropriate behavioral consequences to address misbehavior, such as "time out" or response cost, where a child might lose access to an item of value for a period of time. CBT can also assist parents in better understanding why misbehavior or aggression may be occurring through the use of psychoeducation, and then help them develop a different framework through which to view the behavior in addition to developing a new repertoire of skills to use to address it. CBT also looks at managing family stress and may sometimes assist a parent in identifying and managing their own barriers to effective parenting and behavior management. Sometimes these barriers include a host of parental stressors, such as mental health issues, substance use, or poverty. Parenting a child with significant externalizing behaviors can often exacerbate parental stress, which in turn can make effective parenting even more difficult.

A 2015 meta-analysis of CBT programs (Battagliese et al., 2015) looked at 21 randomized controlled trials which are considered the strongest way to test a treatment. The interventions they examined targeted externalizing behaviors, and included children referred for externalizing symptoms of attention deficit hyperactivity disorder (ADHD), oppositional defiant disorder (ODD), and conduct disorder. Studies were excluded from the analysis if they also included treatment by medication, and so the 21 studies included were therapy only and did not include psychopharmacology. The analysis concluded that CBT programs had a more significant positive effect on the symptoms that were characterized as ODD symptoms than they did on ADHD symptoms. They found that CBT had a significant effect on reducing aggression in children only when parents were involved and not when only the children participated in the programs. They also found that CBT had a significant effect on improving social competence among the populations of children diagnosed with ADHD and ODD; for the children diagnosed with conduct disorder, improvements in social competence were not as robust. Programs that included both children and parents had only a moderate effect on positive parenting, whereas programs that included individual time with parents had a significant effect on positive parenting. There was a large reduction in parental stress when treatment was delivered either to parents and children together or to parents alone. Another interesting secondary outcome was an observed reduction in symptoms of maternal depression, which the authors recommend as a target for future programs given the link between maternal depression and future behavioral problems for children in a household with a depressed mother.

The role of social information processing has been looked at in relation to bullying behavior. For some children who engage in bullying, overly hostile or negative intentions are attributed to the behaviors of others, and so they act in a manner that they perceive as self-protective or defensive, when in fact their reaction is out of proportion to the perceived slight or the slight is wholly inaccurate. Teaching children to more accurately perceive the intentions of others using context and other visible clues can be a helpful way to teach alternative strategies that may be more adaptive in light of the actual situation (Lochman et al., 2012).

The Coping Power program, developed by John Lochman and colleagues (Lochman & Wells, 2002), works to examine social information processing such as in hostile attribution bias as well as more distal factors such as community, parenting, and environmental stressors, which can contribute to aggression. It was originally developed as a 34-session manualized treatment (Lochman & Wells, 2002; Lochman et al., 2012) and was later adapted to promote better implementation and follow-up through addressing barriers to implementation and maintaining gains made in the program.

To this end, helping children and teens identify what they are feeling and why can be incredibly helpful. Teaching children to self-monitor their own internal levels of distress can help lead to the use of strategies such as "stop and think" (Knoff, 2002), which can help them pause before taking further action to consider consequences and make the best choice in response to the trigger.

For many children who act in ways that are experienced as hostile and aggressive, assertive communication may help them better communicate their needs. These children are sometimes lacking the necessary social skills to communicate effectively. This difficulty with assertive, appropriate, and clear communication can limit their abilities to effectively communicate their wants and needs, as well as their emotions. This may pose even more difficulty for boys, who in Western society are typically socialized to more easily express anger than sadness or fear (Brown, 2008).

In group settings, these are sometimes the children who appear to get in trouble frequently such that they then must be removed from their peers and spend time with adults. For children such as this, adults may be "safer" than peers, and even the negative attention from the adult may be preferable to time spent with peers with whom they cannot socialize nor obtain support or connection. This can sometimes derive from a lack of modeled appropriate social behavior in their lives. Some of these children have high levels of social anxiety but do not usually act or behave in a way consistent with the "typical" presentation of a child with anxiety in that they are not withdrawn and do not appear visibly anxious. For children whose behavior and skill set seems to suggest these deficits and possibly some social anxiety, teaching assertive and appropriate communication, as well as improved social skills with peers and others, can help to reduce the desire to be removed from peers and also provide natural reinforcement for more prosocial behavior by way of decreased anxiety and increased positive experiences with others.

There are many high-quality social skills programs that have strong empirical bases of support. These programs can be done at school, at home, or in an outpatient or other clinical setting.

4.3   Family Therapy Models

For nearly all children and adolescents referred for disruptive behavior problems, the most effective treatments address the home and family. Parenting that is coercive, inconsistent, and harsh has been most frequently associated with disorders of conduct in children (Dodge & Pettit, 2003; Frick, 2016). In addition, underlying family stressors can also affect parental stress level and coping skills, and subsequently have great impact on the child who may be the "identified client" of a treatment team. Parent Management Training is a program that has received considerable positive attention and has decades of research support (Colalillo & Johnston, 2016; Kazdin, Siegel, & Bass, 1992).

There are different forms of Parent Management Training curricula and programs but most operate on principles of behavior modification and utilize reinforcement, setting limits with reasonable consequences, and withdrawal of attention in some situations, such as ignoring a toddler's tantrum so as to not reinforce the behavior with attention, even negative attention. Parent training programs look very different at different developmental stages and what is appropriate for a toddler will look very different from the strategies used with adolescents. Although these programs are not specifically targeted at improving the affective states of caregivers, there is some evidence that they may also work to improve feelings of competence and decrease stress, which helps to also improve parenting practice (Colalillo & Johnston, 2016).

Children learn skills they are taught explicitly; however, they also learn from modeling and from observing the behavior of those around them, especially within their home environment. While no parent or caregiver can be expected to be on their best behavior at all times, a parent's own behavior and use of prosocial communication and coping strategies is very important for prosocial development as well as for teaching adaptive coping skills. A parent who tells a child to limit their use of aggressive communication, but is often yelling or cursing at others themselves, is not likely to experience much success.

For preadolescent youth, it is essential that caregivers be involved in treatment, whether as the primary targets or as an adjunctive component to therapy to help support the identified client and help to maintain gains. Different models of parenting have also been identified with more effective prevention of problem behavior in children or with worsening behavior issues in children. Many programs seek to address ineffective or even harmful parenting practices, such as overly coercive or punitive parenting or neglectful parenting.

Many risk factors that accompany poverty and contribute to the severity of a disruptive behavior problem, such as increased stress, less availability to provide supervision, and less external support, can also present barriers to treatment. Difficulties with transportation, communication, and availability can all pose barriers to engaging families in consistent treatment. Therefore, to be effective, a program must have features that can help maintain family engagement and participation in treatment.

4.4   Parent–Child Interaction Therapy

Parent–child interaction therapy (PCIT) is another model of therapy with families that has had very positive results with families of children with a disruptive behavior disorder. PCIT has also been used quite successfully with families referred for physical abuse (Zisser & Eyberg, 2010). Like other therapies that teach more effective and positive methods to respond to challenging behaviors and improve the relationship between parents and child, PCIT teaches and promotes strategies like using praise, active listening, and reflection and calm and consistent delivery of consequences for misbehavior. The parenting style associated with these skills tends to most closely resemble the authoritative style of parenting, first described by Diana Baumrind (1966) in her developmental model. Authoritative parenting is the style that encompasses high levels of expectations, good communication, and high levels of warmth and nurturance. It is associated with a low level of child behavior problems and thought to have the best long-term outcomes for child development.

In PCIT, parents are first taught skills to help establish or strengthen the nurturance and warmth in their relationships through learning to follow their child's lead in play through what is referred to in the method as "child-directed interaction." Once parental responsiveness is increased and the relationship strengthened, then limit setting and consistent discipline are addressed through the teaching and incorporation of "parent-directed interaction." Therapists also work on problem-solving skills with parents to help them effectively manage future behavioral challenges. PCIT is unique in its use of real-time coaching. Parents are taught skills, and then observed while they practice these skills with their children. A PCIT therapist then coaches the parent through the use of an ear bud during the interactions with short statements that may be encouraging of what the parent is doing, (i.e., "Great job with giving specific praise!") or with short redirections once a family has participated in a few sessions and may be more comfortable and less anxious while being coached. Graphs showing their child's progress and weekly skills progress sheets are created and reviewed between therapists and parents. In studies reviewing efficacy, PCIT demonstrated very good results in studies that looked at both significant reductions in child problem behaviors as well as at increased positive interactions between parents and children. In studies of longer term maintenance of treatment gains, families who completed treatment demonstrated continued gains in reduction of disruptive behaviors as well as in maternal parenting confidence (Zisser & Eyberg, 2010).

4.5   Headstart and Early Intervention Programs

Programs that target young children and families who are at risk can be effective in preventing or ameliorating a developmental trajectory that might otherwise lead to child and adolescent behavior problems. These programs can help to address multiple risk factors such as promoting effective parenting practices, addressing parental stress, providing structure and academic and social enrichment and learning for children, and helping families obtain tools to manage childhood behavior problems early on. The Headstart program was developed in the 1965 as part of the "War on Poverty" to help children from impoverished households attain preacademic and other skills prior to starting elementary schools so as to be on par with peers who had more access to high-quality early childhood programs. While initially the program seemed to hold a lot of promise for closing a disparity in academic and social achievement for the children enrolled, more research found that results varied widely from location to location. This was due to differences in factors like teacher and student ratio, and the level of training required for the staff. For the most part, follow-up research found that in many places gains were not maintained beyond a few years once children had completed the program. Investment in quality early intervention and prekindergarten programs has become more of an imperative for states, as evidenced by the move toward tuition-free universal preschool for all children in several cities. Research on the variables that hold the most promise for successful outcomes, both behaviorally and academically, in early childhood programs has pointed to the quality of interaction between the teachers and students (Jacobson, 2008), which is consistent with a more recent focus in K-12 education on classroom and school climate.

4.6   Community-Based In-home Services

In the field of juvenile justice, where the needs of corrections, law enforcement, and mental health come together, the trend has been to maintain youth in their home or community settings whenever possible as a more effective alternative to an out-of-home placement. In addition to the increased effectiveness of intensive, in-home treatment, it is also a cost-saving measure for the local agency paying for it as it is far less costly than an out-of-home placement. Two of the most popular programs that have demonstrated effectiveness through research are functional family therapy (FFT) and multisystemic systems therapy (MST). Both programs seek to address root causes of the youth's behavior difficulties that are occurring at home or in their interactions with their caregivers or family, while then also increasing their network of social support in order to maintain gains and prevent future misbehavior (Devore, 2011).

FFT is a brief, very targeted intervention that typically lasts for only 30 hours or 12 to 14 sessions, and may take place over a three to five month period. The intervention is aimed at 12 to 18 year olds who are considered at risk or delinquent. Therapists work as a team to increase positive and supportive interactions within the family as a means to work toward more effective parenting and support of the child. The program was created in the 1970s by Dr. James F. Alexander (Robbins, Alexander, Turner, & Hollimon, 2016) and is now widely employed by juvenile corrections agencies who utilize it to reduce recidivism. According to the agency now responsible for dissemination of the treatment, FFT is being used in 45 states and 10 countries. There is also some evidence that FFT can be an effective treatment for youth with callous and unemotional traits, who typically do not respond as well to the same treatments, and who may display more problematic behaviors while in treatment (White, Frick, Lawing, & Bauer, 2013). Functional Family Therapy appears to have good results for White youth as well as for Black and Latino youth, who it should be noted, are disproportionately overrepresented in the juvenile justice and residential treatment systems (Darnell & Schuler, 2015; Garbarino, 2015).

Multisystemic therapy (MST), which has the distinction of being rated as a "Model Plus" treatment by the Blueprints initiative (www .blueprintsprograms.com/factsheet/multisystemic-therapy-mst), can be used with 12 to 18 year olds who are the most at risk for an out-of-home placement based on their disruptive behaviors. MST has been used to effectively treat youth with severe antisocial behaviors and is considered most appropriate for those youth who are at risk for incarceration or other out-of-home placements. It is an intensive community and home-based treatment that typically consists of a team of two to four therapists, supervised by an advanced master's or doctoral-level supervisor. Teams also receive weekly consultation from a consultant with MST expertise who helps ensure treatment fidelity and adherence to the model. MST clinicians provide 24-hour/7-day a week availability to help facilitate family participation and also to address crises as they come up in hopes that they can be effectively managed before becoming a significant barrier to treatment. MST was developed to address multiple risk factors across different contexts in recognition that problem behaviors and risk factors interact with and across domains in a child's life. This is partially based on the work of Urie Bronfenbrenner and his social-ecological model (1977). The model looks at various systems and their interactions in a child's life, starting with the youth him/herself, their family and community, and then includes interactions between these systems (i.e., caregivers and school) and the larger systems in which these interactions exist, such as the school system or a caregiver's workplace.

There is also a version of MST specifically for working with juveniles who have committed a sexual offense, MST for Problem Sexual Behaviors, that has shown effectiveness with this population. MST, which like FFT also has a team of therapists working in the home, is more intensive in that there are multiple sessions per week. Therapists in this model also work on strengthening family relationships and community support, but will work directly with family members on any barriers to treatment, such as a parent's own substance abuse or mental health issues. Therapists from MST may attend meetings with a parent at school, assist a parent in obtaining their own substance abuse treatment if they relapse, and also assist with some clinical case management.

In the continuum of behavioral health services for children, a residential treatment facility (RTF) is a highly restrictive setting, intended for children who have not responded sufficiently to outpatient therapy or other types of community or home-based mental health. Children typically attend school and receive individual, group, and milieu therapy while at an RTF. Most facilities also include family therapy; however, there may be significant barriers to family participation. These can include geographical limits as well as general disengagement from treatment. It has been the experience of these writers, both of whom have spent a portion of their careers in RTF work, that very often when a child is admitted to an RTF, the family seems to rather quickly reorganize in the child's absence, even if perhaps often not intentionally. A study published in 2016 by Patterson, Dulmus, Maguin, and Perkins, looked at differences in outcomes for youth of ethnic and racial minority status and youth of majority status in residential treatment and found the significant disparities existed. Minority youth did not respond as well in treatment and had a lower rate of being successfully discharged when compared to their White and majority counterparts. Also, alarming is the use of seclusion and restraint in residential settings despite the movement nationally to reduce and eliminate their use in schools and in other treatment settings. A 2015 study found that out of 693 residential facilities surveyed, 82% reported the use of seclusion and restraint. The authors found that the practice was more frequent at larger, privately run facilities that receive public funding (Green-Hennessy & Hennessy 2015).

In most locations throughout the country, there has been a shift away from the overutilization of RTF treatment in recent years, and certainly away from lengthy stays in RTFs, and toward more community and home-based interventions, such as those described above. RTFs will continue to serve an important role on the treatment continuum for youth who cannot be maintained safely in their homes and communities; however, the use of this level of care should be judicious both for the admission and length of stay. While the behavior modification programs and other treatments in residential settings may serve clients well while they are there, the gains made in treatment do not always generalize to the home and community setting where the child will inevitably return. When the child's behavior at home or school is most problematic, then it is crucial that family be heavily involved in both treatment and both family and school staff be involved in discharge planning and aftercare coordination with any aftercare service providers. To this end, many RTF providers now heavily emphasize family engagement from the point of admission through discharge by holding frequent family sessions at times and places convenient to the family whenever possible, often conducting a portion of the child's treatment in the child's home or community when geographically feasible, and allowing for ample home passes and visits unlike the "blackout" periods often a part of the RTF protocols of the past in which youth were disconnected from their families for a period of time following admission and sometimes following negative behavior.

4.7   Group Therapy Models

Some earlier work looking into group therapy for youth with antisocial behaviors found that not only were groups ineffective for these youth but that they actually could cause harm through iatrogenic effects. The idea behind this was that by having young people with severe antisocial behaviors pulled out of the mainstream and then placed in groups together, they might learn worse behavior, or engage in "deviancy training" while together if in a group setting that was too unstructured, such as in a process group (Gifford-Smith, Dodge, Dishion, & McCord, 2005;

Sawyer, Borduin, & Dopp, 2015). The guiding principal behind this is that friendships and associations with other peers with conduct problems can exacerbate the symptoms of both. This viewpoint is echoed in many juvenile probation offices that prohibit youth on probation to spent time with other youth on probation; being out with other juveniles who are also on probation can constitute a violation of one's probation in many counties. A recent meta-analysis also found less effectiveness for groups that had primarily male adolescents with significant behavior problems; however, the study did find that group interventions may be of benefit for prevention purposes in younger children (Sawyer et al., 2015).

4.8   Applied Behavior Analysis and Behaviorism

Applied behavior analysis (ABA) has been associated with successful outcomes for children with autism but can also be successfully applied to other behavior issues. Children who have limited ability to use insight either because they are too young or developmentally or cognitively impaired can especially benefit from a more behaviorally based program of therapy. ABA, which is based upon the operant conditioning work of B. F. Skinner, can be effective for addressing disruptive behavior problems, especially in the context of younger children or children who are less communicative. Operant conditioning is based on the premise that any condition which increases the likelihood of a behavior increasing in frequency is a reinforcer and any condition or consequence which decreases the likelihood of a behavior occurring is considered to be a punishment. Thus, behaviors can be increased, diminished, or extinguished through the use of teaching and manipulation of reinforcing or punishing agents. Operationally defining the behavior is the first step toward observation and data gathering around the antecedents and possibly triggers of the behavior. When formulating hypotheses about the function of a behavior, it is also important to obtain data on the frequency, severity, and duration of the behavior. Obtaining objective data on a child's behavior can also be a helpful exercise in and of itself. When child misbehavior is characterized in subjective or hazy terms, such as "Joe is acting up," "Susie is being manipulative," or "Luke is out of control," it is important to clarify concerns in terms of objective and observable terms, such as "Joe threw a chair in class this morning," "Susie lied about her whereabouts twice last week," or "Luke had a tantrum this afternoon which lasted for five minutes, and one yesterday which lasted for three minutes." It is often helpful for an outside consultant to observe a situation in order to collect data on antecedents and consequences of behavior which may be much less apparent to the teacher or caregiver engaged in the situation with the child.

In a broader sense, if one accepts the behaviorism-based premise that all behaviors serve a purpose, even if it doesn't appear to be particularly helpful to the child, then behaviors which are problematic not only need to be unlearned or extinguished, but replaced with more prosocial behaviors which may fulfill the same purpose or meet the need in another way. If a behavior that had served a purpose, such as using aggressive communication to get one's needs met, is unlearned, then gains will not be maintained unless a suitable replacement is taught; in this example asking for things in a more appropriate but clear way, which can be accomplished through teaching assertive communication skills. For this reason, it is important to understand what need or function the target behavior serves.

In the case of children who act out in sexually inappropriate ways, part of CBT for this population includes working with a client to identify the internal and external triggers which are associated with the problem behavior, and then coming up with alternative behaviors to engage in when facing a potentially triggering situation. For children who act in physically violent or sexually inappropriate ways, it may be important to teach other ways to gain physical contact, such as approved "OK" touches which may include high fives, hugs (depending on the setting), or other physical stimulation or attention. Misbehavior that results in a child's removal from a classroom setting may serve an alternate purpose, such as escaping academic demands, social demands, or gaining access to a preferred activity or item.

One of the writers once observed in the office of an elementary school setting that one particular 7th grade student who was considered a troublemaker was "punished" for his aggressive and defiant behavior in class by being asked to leave the classroom. When he would leave the classroom, he would usually be sent to the dean of students, who then would spend copious amounts of one-on-one time with this student, sometimes reading him books or just having lengthy conversations. In his classroom, which was often chaotic, he did not receive the same level of attention and he often was unable to receive the academic support he badly needed. Sometimes this student would be simply sitting in the main office, waiting for the dean. On another occasion, this student and a group of three other boys, who had also been asked to leave the class and go to see the dean because of misbehavior, were observed watching a rather sexually explicit video on the computer of the dean of students after she had left her office door open while she was at a meeting, and told the boys she would be back soon to see them. In this situation, it quickly became clear that this student's need for attention as well as his need for a strong relationship with an adult was likely reinforcing his defiance and misbehavior. Some academic testing also revealed that he was far behind and likely also was able to avoid feelings of shame or frustration by leaving the room and missing instructional time. In this child's case, a plan was devised in which in addition to receiving more individualized academic support, his visits and time spent with the dean of students was contingent upon his improved behavior and use of appropriate communication skills; additionally, this time had to be supervised and some supervision guidelines were put into place in order to avoid students using administrative offices in the absence of an adult to watch explicit videos! It is not uncommon for teachers to use "lunch with the teacher" as an incentive for improved behavior so as to help meet attention needs of children. In coming up with strategies to address these needs, the function of the behavior has to be determined and in doing so, ABA provides an effective tool. Additionally, comparing behavioral data before and after an intervention provides useful guidance as to whether the behavioral intervention helped and if so, whether it should be continued, tapered, or otherwise altered.

4.9   Trauma-focused Therapy

In cases in which children are reacting to a traumatic event with externalizing behaviors, trauma is best treated by trauma-focused therapy. This may be concurrent with other interventions aimed at reducing behavior problems. It is not uncommon for children who have experienced trauma, particularly repetitive traumatic events, to behave in ways that recreates that trauma in their lives. For instance, young people who grew up with adults abusing, mistreating, or rejecting them may continue to behave in ways that elicit these reactions from others and young people who grew up in violent and chaotic homes may continue to exhibit aggressive and disruptive behaviors, because a violent and chaotic environment feels safest for its familiarity.

In the case of a child who has experienced a traumatic event and evidences traumatic stress along with behavior problems in school or home, there is sometimes a reticence on the part of caregivers, teachers, and school staff to address behavior problems or even to enforce household or classroom rules in fear of overwhelming the child at a time when they seem most emotionally vulnerable. However, in the case of boundaries and limits at home, restoring a sense of normalcy and routine after a traumatic event can be incredibly beneficial, provided that the discipline and boundaries are appropriately set and enforced. For a child who has experienced a destabilizing event, walking into a classroom where the rules are predictable and reasonable, and the adult(s) in the room are supportive and stable, can greatly aid in recovery. Conversely, a traumatized child who attends a school that is chaotic, overly punitive and where the relationships between adults and students are mistrusting or cold, has the potential to be further derailed by these factors.

Considered one of the most effective, evidence-based treatments for trauma, Trauma-Focused CBT (Cohen, Mannarino, & Deblinger, 2006) is generally the treatment of choice for children and adolescents who have experienced trauma. The treatment utilizes a CBT model that includes emotional identification and regulation, cognitive coping and relaxation skills, psychoeducation about trauma and other related issues (i.e., the range of feelings and physical reactions children can have after a traumatic event), and gradual exposure, leading up to the creation of a trauma narrative by the client, which is then ideally shared with a caregiver in therapy. Trauma-Focused CBT includes caregiver and family components such that adults are also engaged in treatment with their children to support their children, gain assistance, and support around managing any behavioral difficulties in their children as well as to identify their own reactions to the trauma, which can impact greatly on the recovery of their child, especially when the child is young.

Trauma-Focused CBT also includes a component of "body safety" to further promote safety skills to ideally reduce future vulnerability to abuse or other potentially destabilizing events through teaching and modeling skills such as "No, go, tell" where a child can practice alerting an adult if they need immediate help from a potentially unsafe situation. This component may also include providing developmentally appropriate sexual education. There is also a specialized Trauma-Focused CBT protocol to treat traumatic grief in children and adolescents (Cohen et al., 2006).

Other evidence-based treatments that are being utilized and disseminated for treating trauma in children include Prolonged Exposure Therapy (Foa, Chrestman, & Gilboa-Schechtman, 2009). Like Trauma-Focused CBT, this also utilizes a model of anxiety reduction through exposure, but is more behavioral in its direct versus gradual approach of exposure to the thoughts and feelings around the traumatic event. Initially Prolonged Exposure was only utilized with adults. In recent years, it has been adapted for use with adolescents and children, with success (Foa et al., 2009).

Eye Movement Desensitization and Reprocessing therapy (EMDR) has also had promising results and in some studies has proven as effective at reducing symptoms of post-traumatic stress disorder (PTSD) as CBT treatments (Diehle, Opmeer, Boer, Mannarino, & Lindauer, 2015). EMDR would appear to also benefit children who are young or otherwise less able to communicate verbally. EMDR should only be practiced by those who have received specialized training in the technique.

It is important that a clinician work with a family on strategies to manage behavioral issues concurrently with therapy that focused on recovery from the trauma. While it is important to use an evidence-based, trauma-focused treatment to address symptoms of traumatic stress, research has shown that the single most important factor in a child's recovery from trauma is the support of a caring and stable adult, ideally a primary caregiver (Cohen et al., 2006).

In recent years, our understanding of what may cause a traumatic stress response has expanded. Trauma is not necessarily a discrete event or set of circumstances but can also consist of repeated exposure or knowledge of violence, or of prolonged inadequate care. In the most recent version of the *DSM-5* (American Psychiatric Association, 2013), the definition of PTSD included expanded criteria for what constitutes a trauma to include being witness to a traumatic event or even learning about a traumatic event that happened to a loved one.

4.10   Disruptive Behavior Problems and Attachment

Children and adolescents who meet criteria for a diagnosis of reactive attachment disorder (RAD) or developmental attachment disorder (DAD) often also display behavior which can be described as oppositional or defiant. Accurate estimates of the prevalence of RAD are not readily available; a 1994 study by Richters and Volkmar put RAD at a prevalence of 1% of the population, but among samples of children who have entered the foster care system after being abused or having been raised previously in an institution, the rates seem to vary between 33% to as high as 40% ("Practice Parameter," 2005).

In some cases, children with RAD have been described as having trust issues as a result of problematic attachments with caregivers, and as a result may function in a way that ranges from being described as manipulative and controlling to alarmingly aggressive. In a report by the American Professional Society on the Abuse of Children (APSAC) on the treatment of attachment disorders and some of the attendant controversial therapies, the authors write, "Children described as having attachment problems are alleged by proponents of the controversial therapies to be at risk for becoming psychopaths who will go on to engage in very serious delinquent, criminal, and antisocial behaviors if left untreated" (Chaffin et al., 2006, p. 78).

For children who may have attachment issues undergirding their behavioral difficulties, or for children and adolescents who may even meet full criteria for a diagnosis of RAD and display problematic disruptive behaviors, caution must be taken not to engage in any of the nonevidence-based treatments which have not only been proven to be in-effective, but which have actually been shown to cause harm, sometimes fatal. "Rebirthing" and other controversial practices which have fallen under the broad umbrella of "attachment parenting" have resulted in the deaths of children whose families claimed to be following the advice of experts in the area (Chaffin et al., 2006).

The 2005 "Practice Parameter for the Assessment and Treatment of Children and Adolescents With Reactive Attachment Disorder of Infancy and Early Childhood" guidelines from the Academy of Child and Adolescent Psychiatry caution clinicians to look more closely at areas of difficulty, which often include conduct and oppositionality. They support adjunctive treatments targeted at children with RAD who have also been diagnosed or appear to show signs of ODD or conduct disorder, such as MST or parent management training, and advise that families should avoid "Interventions Designed to Enhance Attachment that Involve Noncontingent Physical Restraint or Coercion (e.g., 'Therapeutic Holding' or 'Compression Holding'), Reworking of Trauma (e.g., 'Rebirthing Therapy'), or Promotion of Regression for 'Reattachment'" ("Practice Parameter," 2005 p. 1216), since these therapies have no empirical support and can cause serious harm including death. Instead, caregivers and clinicians are recommended to consider the specific needs of the child presenting with RAD and use non-coercive positive approaches to addressing attachment and trust related issues.

4.11   Kleptomania and Pyromania

Kleptomania may have similar neural pathways to other behavioral addictions, such as compulsive gambling, and the neurotransmitters dopamine, serotonin, and the opioid systems are thought to play a role. There is promise for medications that act on these neurotransmitters, such as Selective Serotonin Reuptake Inhibitors (SSRIs), or medications that act on opioid receptors. CBT is currently the treatment of choice for Kleptomania in adults (Dannon, Aizer, & Lowengrub, 2006); however, there is far less research in this area for youth. Kleptomania can be viewed primarily as a disorder of impulse control, and so the techniques used to treat it work to reduce or manage the impulse to steal (Grant & Kim, 2002). It can also be argued that Kleptomania more closely resembles obsessive–compulsive disorder, and can be treated similarly. Flouxetine (brand name Prozac ©) has been effective at treating Obsessive Compulsive Disorder (Dannon et al., 2006) and this, or another SSRI, may be considered for treatment of Kleptomania.

Pyromania can also be viewed as a disorder of impulse control primarily. In addition to CBT, psychoeducation explicitly given around fire safety has been found to be helpful. A study comparing CBT and Fire Safety Education found that each treatment had their merits both when combined and apart but suggest that the efficacy of each may depend more on the characteristics of the clients and the variables being examined (Kolko, Herschell, & Scharf, 2006).

4.12   Psychopharmacology

Psychopharmacology can be most helpful when used in conjunction with therapeutic treatment, and can help to ameliorate symptoms, but should not be an intervention unto itself for a disruptive behavior disorder ("Practice Parameter," 2007). There is no one psychopharmacological treatment recommended for disruptive behavior problems. In part, this reflects the heterogeneity of behavior and conduct problems and the reasons why they occur. In the case of disruptive behavior disorders, psychopharmacology can help to treat or manage symptoms, primarily those of aggression or impulse control, but not the underlying causes of the disorder itself. Aggression can occur as a result of conduct disorders, impulse control disorders, developmental disabilities, posttraumatic stress, a manic episode, a psychotic break, or ADHD, in addition to some highly context dependent situations. As a result, it is important for any root causes to be examined at the onset of any psychopharmacological treatment (Mehler-Wex, Romanos, & Warnke, 2014).

When conduct disorder or ODD co-occurs with another disorder such as ADHD, psychotherapy is recommended as the first line of treatment, with psychopharmacology recommended only for treatment-resistant cases (Ipser & Stein, 2007). However, in a 2007 meta-analysis of different randomized controlled trials for psychopharmacology for disruptive behavior disorders, Ipser and Stein found that stimulant medication, in this case usually Methylphenidate (the generic version of Ritalin ©), had demonstrated effectiveness for boys who were impulsive and who also demonstrated aggression. The medication was linked to a reduction in both impulsivity and in aggression. Stimulants are generally supported as a medication treatment of first choice for children who present with aggression as a result of ADHD or impulse control difficulties.

In recent years, there has been a noted increase in the use of what are referred to as second or third generation, or "atypical," antipsychotics to treat behavior and mood issues in children and adolescents. What were once considered to be "off label" uses for these medications are now widely accepted for the treatment of aggression and other behavior problems in adolescents and teenagers. Atypical antipsychotics such as Aripiprazole (better known by the brand name Abilify ©), Risperidone (brand name

Risperdal ©), Olanzapine (brand name Zyprexa ©), and Quetiapine (brand name Seroquel ©) pose a lower risk of side effects such as tardive dyskinesia when compared to the "traditional" antipsychotic (Mehler-Wex et al., 2014) medications such as Haloperidol (brand name Haldol ©) and Ziprasidone (brand name Geodon ©) or Chlorpromazine (brand name Thorazine ©). These first-generation antipsychotics are sometimes used when there is an instance of acute aggression that needs to be stopped immediately and other types of restraints have been tried and are unsuccessful, but only on an as-needed basis and generally not as part of a longer term medication regimen due to concerns about adverse side effects. Mood stabilizers and anticonvulsants, such as carbamazepine (brand name Tegretol ©), gabapentin (brand name Neurontin ©), lamotrigine (brand name Lamictal ©), oxcarbazepine (brand name Trileptal ©), and valproic acid (brand name Depakote ©), have also had an increase in being used to treat aggression and have shown some positive effects, but are still not considered the psychopharmacological treatment of first choice. The effects for mood stabilizers are mixed and the potential for physical harm is great with some mood stabilizers, particularly lithium salts. In multiple double-blind, controlled studies, lithium was shown to be effective in treating adolescents with comorbid ADHD, conduct disorder, and ODD, but lithium salts are generally not advised for children under 12 years, and when prescribed, lithium salts should only be prescribed where compliance and medical monitoring can be assured (Mehler-Wex et al., 2014). Benzodiazepenes, which are used for anxiety, can also be used to treat aggression; however, due to their highly addictive nature, use is recommended to be short term (Mehler-Wex et al., 2014).

The Ipser and Stein meta-analysis (2007) found that Risperidone (the generic version of Risperdal ©) was effective at treating aggressive symptoms, especially when combined with a stimulant, but do note that in addition to the short-term side effects, which can include weight gain, sleepiness, and in some cases, lactation, long-term effects are not well known yet. A 2015 study of neurological side effects in children using atypical antipsychotics found that after a year of follow-up and monitoring, there were significantly higher rates of movement disorders, known as dyskinesias, in children treated with risperidone than with quetiapine. They also found higher rates of parkinsonism, referring to the tremors and stiffening that can occur in

Parkinson's disease, in children treated with risperidone or olanzapine than with quetiapine at follow-up. Among the risk factors which seemed to increase the odds of developing these symptoms were young age and time spent taking the medication. The authors also caution that the social effects of these movement disorders could cause very problematic social problems for children at a time when developing peer relationships is very important, and vulnerability to social isolation and peer harassment increases (Garcia-Amador et al., 2015).

In considering psychopharmacological treatments for adolescents and children, one needs to weigh the efficacy of the drug against potential side effects which can not only affect behavior and cause visible movement and neurological impairment, but which may have medical consequences which are not visible such as impacting kidney and liver function. When treating a child or adolescent taking atypical antipsychotics, a clinician must be very attentive to any changes in behavior or functioning that can be signs of side effects and must be attended to quickly. Among the most serious side effect is the development of Neuroleptic Malignant Syndrome, which can result from antipsychotic medications and neuroleptics. The symptoms of this are a high fever, sweating, unstable blood pressure, stupor, muscular rigidity, and autonomic dysfunction. If these symptoms develop, then the client should be referred for immediate medical treatment and the psychotropic medication should be immediately stopped.

Another problem which can develop is that of anticholinergic syndrome, which is more commonly associated with medications in the elderly, but which can occur in children and adolescents as well. These occur when medications block the neurotransmitter acetylcholine in the body. This can often result in dehydration which in turn can cause severe constipation. Other symptoms include loss of muscle control which can include tremors and enuresis, as well as confusion and dizziness (Whitaker & Rao, 1992). Some adolescents are prescribed multiple medications, included those given on an as-needed basis such as Benedryl, which can all contribute to these effects.

A recent study (Olfson, King, & Schoenbaum, 2015) looked at the rates of prescriptions of psychotropic medications for children from 2006 to 2009 and found that the rates of prescription for children under 12 years had declined, but during this same time period, had increased for children over 12 years of age. Of concern is that most of the children and adolescents receiving these medications were not prescribed them by a psychiatric provider. Although some have argued for increased support for pediatric psychotropic use, there is a need for more long-term safety and efficacy studies of existing medications and newer, safer, and more effective agents with fewer side effects for the pharmacological treatment of all childhood disorders in which aggression is prominent (Nevels, Dehon, Alexander, & Gontkovsky, 2010).

4.13   Addressing Moral Panic: Effective and Ineffective Policy and School Programs for Youth With Challenging Behaviors

The link between child mental health, school success (or lack thereof), and negative adult trajectories, such as delinquency, substance abuse, or other problems, cannot be overstated. Students who do not complete high school comprise a larger percentage of adults who are institutionalized and are at greater risk for delinquency. Children who do not graduate from high school in the United States are more likely to experience reduced job and income opportunities as adults, earning significantly less over their lifetimes than their peers who have graduated from high school or who attain a college degree, and as a result, are at greater risk for the negative outcomes which can accompany poverty in the United States, including housing instability, inadequate health care and worse physical health outcomes (Adams, 2015; American Psychological Association [APA], 2012).

In their 2012 report on the issue of American youth who drop out of school, the American Psychological Association stated:

> The risk of incarceration (jails, prisons, juvenile detention centers) for male dropouts is significant. In 2007, male dropouts aged 16-24 were 6.3 times more likely to be institutionalized than high school graduates and when compared with those with a bachelor degree or higher, their risk skyrocketed to 63 times more likely, according to the Center for Labor Market Studies (2009).

(American Psychological Association, 2012, p. 6)

For children who identified as lesbian, gay, bisexual, or transgender (LGBT), the risk of dropping out is even higher due to peer aggression and a hostile school climate. In 2008, students who identified as LGBT were three times more likely than their non-LGBT peers to drop out of school (APA, 2012). At the same time, nearly 9 out of 10 LGBT students surveyed reported that they had experienced harassment or bullying sometime in the past year, and so interventions targeted at LGBT youth school completion have targeted school climate and bullying policies.

As to how race and poverty factor into the equation of dropout risk, the APA goes on to say:

> Several risk factors affect children born at the intersection of race and poverty throughout their development predicting school failure or dropout and entry into the juvenile justice system. Children of color struggling academically or acting out are often met with police intervention, suspensions, or expulsions instead of appropriate academic intervention in schools of poor quality (Children's Defense Fund, 2007). African American students in particular are disciplined or suspended at disproportionate rates for reasons that include lack of teacher training (in classroom management or culturally competent practices) and racial stereotypes only contributing further to disengagement and later dropout from school ("Are Zero Tolerance Policies Effective?", 2008). (APA, 2012, pp. 4–5)

While the dropout rates for students with disabilities decreased from 45.9% to 26.2% from the 1995 to 1996 school year to the 2005 to 2006 school year (U.S. Department of Education, 2011, as cited in APA 2012), the data showed that of the students with disabilities who did drop out, the group that numbered the highest (44%) were those students who were classified as receiving school-based services under the category "emotional disturbance" (APA, 2012). Students who meet criteria for a diagnosis of ODD or another impulse control or behavioral dysregulation disorder are most often classified under "emotional disturbance" and sometimes placed in self-contained classrooms apart from the general education population. The IDEA of 1997, reauthorized in 2004, emphasizes the principle of "Least Restrictive Environment" in special education placement (Hosp & Reschly, 2002). This federal act and subsequent case law establishes that children who meet criteria for special education should always be placed with their peers in a regular education setting with supports, versus a self-contained classroom or in a self-contained school, when possible. Typically, the placement of African American students who were classified as meeting criteria for "emotional disturbance" in self-contained classrooms has been significantly higher than the placement of their White peers who are receiving services for the same classification (Hosp & Reschly, 2002; Skiba, 2014).

For a given child with behavioral difficulties, where they are born, what kind of school they attend, and their family's race and socioeconomic status can greatly influence what type of support they receive and also determine their developmental trajectory. This becomes especially apparent when considering the route from student to "drop out" or delinquent.

"Zero Tolerance" is a school discipline policy which originated during the Reagan administration in the 1980s, in tandem with renewed efforts to reduce drug abuse in American youth by adopting what were seen as "tough on crime" policies (APA, 2012; Skiba, 2014). "Zero Tolerance," which is partly based on the "Broken Windows" policing theory, attempts to address serious student infractions through punishing far less severe infractions, such as dressing inappropriately, using a cellphone during class, using disrespectful language, and other school offenses which had traditionally not warranted an out-of-school suspension or intervention from law enforcement. After the shooting at Columbine High School and other high-profile shootings in the 1990s, support for these kinds of policies increased among a general public, even though at the time, school shootings were a high intensity but low frequency event. Most offenses in schools who have adopted these policies result in suspensions, expulsions, arrests, or other measures which keep children out of instructional time. The results of "Zero Tolerance" policies, which have come under greater scrutiny in the last 10 years or so, were that they were inconsistently applied, ineffective, and even harmful to the students and communities they were designed to support. An examination of the data around "Zero Tolerance" demonstrates that there was not a resultant reduction in school violence, and that in fact, suspensions and expulsions can increase negative outcomes for students, negatively impact school climate, and act as a means to "push out" certain students, disproportionality impacting students of color, students living in poverty, and students with disabilities. ("Are Zero Tolerance Policies Effective?", 2008; Skiba, 2014). In his summary of the research on this, Skiba also points out that ridding a school of perceived "troublemakers" did not improve school climate but actually made it worse in the eyes of students, parents, and teachers.

Students of color, students from areas of high poverty, and students with disabilities are also disproportionately affected by what has been termed the "School to Prison Pipeline." This refers to an increased utilization of local law enforcement in school settings and ultimately an increase in the numbers of youth who end up in adult penal system as a result of school infractions. In 2014, the United States had the highest incarceration rate in the world, at a rate of 698 per 10,000 people (The Sentencing Project, 2015), at tremendous cost to society. The report goes on to show that while the number of youth sent to secure residential facilities through the juvenile justice system has steadily declined, from a peak 77,800 in 1999 to 35,200 in 2013, youth of color are still committed at a higher rate and given more severe punishments than their White peers (The Sentencing Project, 2015).

As we examine the data and overly punitive and ineffective policies come under greater scrutiny, there is hope of more research-based solutions being enacted in schools to stem the "school to prison pipeline." When one considers that many of the infractions which result in suspension or arrest start off as behavioral incidents that can be de-escalated or otherwise safely managed by trained staff and appropriate in school supports, it becomes essential to implement best practice in schools.

4.14   Mental Health Delivery in School Settings

It has been estimated that nearly 80% of all mental health services for children are delivered in a school setting (Rones & Hogwood, 2000). Best practice in mental health provision in schools is both evidence based and in compliance with state and federal guidelines around special education and mental health. The use of Positive Behavior Supports and Functional Analyses to address behavior issues are specifically mentioned in IDEA and the

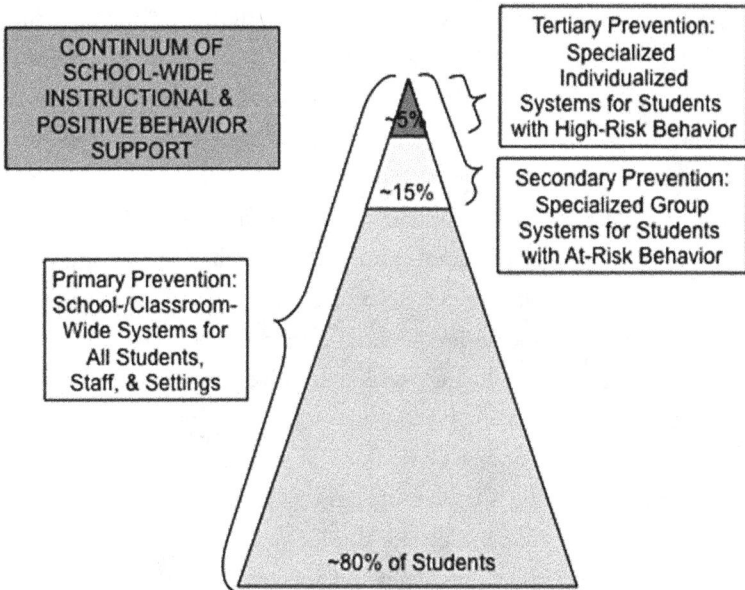

CONTINUUM OF SCHOOL-WIDE INSTRUCTIONAL & POSITIVE BEHAVIOR SUPPORT

Tertiary Prevention:
Specialized
Individualized
Systems for Students
with High-Risk Behavior

~5%

Secondary Prevention:
Specialized Group
Systems for Students
with At-Risk Behavior

~15%

Primary Prevention:
School-/Classroom-
Wide Systems for
All Students,
Staff, & Settings

~80% of Students

Source: OSEP Center on PBIS, United States Department of Education, 2010, p. 20

language was kept in after the 2004 reauthorization, making these practices part of a federal mandate for school districts (Office of Special Education Program [OSEP] Center on Positive Behavior Interventions and Supports [PBIS], United States Department of Education, 2010). Schoolwide positive behavioral support (SWPBS) is a model that has received positive attention in trying to address the overuse of suspension and expulsion from schools and ultimately disrupt the "school to prison pipeline." SWPBS utilizes a multitiered system of support for students at various levels of behavioral severity, from schoolwide prevention programs that enhance outcomes for all students to more individually designed interventions targeting the children who do not respond at lower levels of support. SWPBS also utilizes increased accountability through data collection.

This model represents a collection of best practices that are supported by research, with an eye toward prevention, support of students through teaching new skills, and alternatives to school expulsion, suspension, or arrest as interventions.

Group interventions that have empirical support for preventing behavior can be implemented at the classroomwide level. One of the best supported interventions of this kind for young children is "The Incredible Years" (Webster-Stratton & Reid, 2007), which consists of a series of interventions targeting children, caregivers, and classroom teachers at different age groups. The program for school-aged children (ages 6 to 12 years) has a classroom group intervention component as well as a parent component and has been in use since the 1980s. The program aims to increase protective factors and prosocial behaviors in children by strengthening parent and teacher relationships, helping children increase their self-regulation, and aiding in better classroom management practice for teachers, while also reducing possible negative outcomes and by doing so, improving developmental pathways as children age. The classroom intervention piece is a social-emotional skills curriculum that utilizes dinosaur puppets. There is also a more targeted intervention for families of children who appear to demonstrate conduct problems which has shown success in reducing conduct problems and possibly in reducing longer term negative outcomes. In a 2011 study published by Webster-Stratton and her team, in a sample of children and their caregivers who had participated in the targeted program when their children were three to eight years of age, nearly 85% of the sample appeared to maintain their postintervention gains. The outcome measures examined in the long-term follow-up study included markers of later developmental markers than can result from early childhood conduct problems, such as juvenile delinquency, substance use, and psychological adjustment (Webster-Stratton, Rinaldi, & Reid, 2011).

The use of functional behavior analysis (FBA) can help to determine the cause of an individual's behavior by looking at antecedents and consequences of the behavior and carefully examining the setting and conditions in which it occurs to best determine what is maintaining it (Zirkel, 2011). Based on principles of behaviorism, it is instrumental in then designing an individualized behavior plan for a child. This tool is based on principles of manipulating one's environment in order to get the desired behavioral change. It can be used in conjunction with other interventions. Traditionally, many think of FBAs as being tools for children on the autism spectrum but they can and should be utilized in trying to design a plan for a student or classroom where behavioral issues are getting in the way of learning.

Another promising intervention for schools is that of Restorative Justice. This approach involves coming together in dialogue in order to restore harmony to a community and was primarily utilized in the juvenile justice and criminal justice systems until recently, when more schools have tried to adapt it (Ortega, Lyubansky, Nettles, & Espelage, 2016). This method holds promise as an alternative to traditional and more hierarchal school discipline approaches, and takes the school as a community into account. There is limited research on its effectiveness, but more studies are underway to help determine its effectiveness as either part of a more comprehensive approach to school discipline such as PBIS or a stand-alone approach (Hurley, Guckenberg, Persson, Fronius, & Petrosino, 2015).

4.15   Cultural Competence in Treatment

Treatment that is culturally competent respectfully considers the multiple identities of a given client. Treatment can be most effective when factors such as gender identity, sexual orientation, ethnic and racial background, ability status, religious beliefs and faith traditions (or lack thereof), acculturation and second language learner status, can be integrated into treatment. In addition, the individual values and beliefs of a given family and child must be taken into account; the culturally competent therapist takes care not to apply cultural knowledge about a given group to an individual client without first understanding how much this knowledge applies to a given person and their own experience. An example of this would be a therapist who has read a client's chart prior to meeting and noting that they appear to be of Latino descent, begins an introductory session by emphasizing perceived Latino values without learning more about the family and their level of identification with any of these values.

Conversely, therapists can make the mistake of being "color blind" which can lead to a lack of acknowledgement of important cultural or ethnic variables that influence how a family may view treatment or view the issues which have brought them into treatment. Families from different cultures can have widely variable expectations for their children and the role of children in the immediate and extended family. When working with a family with a child referred to treatment for a disruptive behavior problem, it is crucial to assess and understand how the family views the behavior. It is also crucial to understand how the family views the opinions of others who have either worked with the child or the family who may be experiencing the child's behavior differently.

If working with a family or child who has fled an area with civil war or tribal conflict, it is important to ensure that any translators do not come from the warring side of the conflict. A common belief about cultural competence is that it is optimal for a treating therapist to be of the same ethnic and racial makeup as the client, but research on this has shown that a culturally competent therapist of any ethnic background is a more important factor in recovery than is racial or ethnic matching (Leong & Gupta, 2008). Some treatment protocols place a specific emphasis on the importance of the therapist understanding, respecting, and actively utilizing family culture in treatment, including embracing the family's definition or view of the problems that brought them to therapy. For instance, in FFT this is referred to as "matching," although this does not have the same connotation as specifically matching families and therapists who share a racial or ethnic identity. Of course, while it is not unusual for individuals and families to express preference for working with therapists with similar cultural background or with those who are very knowledgeable about the unique concerns that may be associated with the ways the family identifies or individuals in the family identify, no therapist can be truly fluent in the culture of each family or individual with which he or she interacts. This is especially true when one considers that culture is fluid and ever changing, not a fixed set of factors that can ever be mastered, and even among people who identify the same way racially, ethnically, or religiously, or who seem to identify similarly in other ways, cultural experience may be similar, but never identical. For these reasons, the concept of "cultural humility" has been emerging in more recent years. Cultural humility refers to a person's willingness and ability, in this case that of the clinician, to be self-reflective by acknowledging the limits of one's own knowledge and understanding, and to be flexible and receptive to learning from the individuals and families with which the clinician works (Tervalon & Murray-Garcia, 1998). Cultural humility in therapy helps to better understand the meaning that a client makes for him/herself and in doing so, can help guide treatment.

CHAPTER 5

Case Studies

Case Study 1

Amanda

Amanda was a 11-year-old female who was admitted to residential treatment after it was discovered that she made multiple attempts to harm her mother through means such as poisoning her drinks and food and placing items in the shower and outside her mother's bedroom door that caused her to slip and fall. Amanda had not received any behavioral health treatment prior to her admission for residential treatment. However, due to the multiple significant attempts she made to harm her mother in addition to other problem behaviors reported at the time of her first contact with the mental health system—including stealing and animal cruelty—residential treatment was authorized.

Amanda's parents had recently separated at the time of Amanda's admission to residential treatment, which was their fourth separation during Amanda's lifetime. Amanda's father was reportedly diagnosed with Bipolar Disorder and frequently stopped taking his prescribed medications during which time he frequently became violent and destructive. Amanda's mother reported that Amanda had been exposed to domestic violence in the home throughout her life. According to Amanda's mother, Amanda's father often destroyed items in the home, including televisions and furniture, and hit, pushed, slapped, punched, and pulled Amanda's mother's hair. These incidents contributed to the multiple marital separations, and Amanda's mother noted that Amanda would express a longing to be with her father during the separations and blamed Amanda's mother for making her father leave the home. Amanda was surprisingly open at the start of residential treatment in acknowledging that she had attempted to harm her mother. Amanda offered her view point that her mother was at fault for her father leaving the home and her concern that she would lose contact with her father. She explained that she wanted to harm her mother so she could live with her father. Although Amanda's father reported wanting to be part of her treatment, he appeared for visits only, not for the intake or treatment sessions.

Amanda's mother reported that Amanda was born full-term and healthy, but was difficult to soothe as an infant and toddler and often appeared unhappy. Amanda's mother initially reported that Amanda's problem behaviors had developed only recently, but as treatment progressed it became more apparent that although the behavior problems had intensified recently, Amanda had a history of conduct problems from around the time she started school. Amanda's mother eventually acknowledged that she began receiving reports from Amanda's teachers about Amanda stealing peers' belongings around age six. During parent–teacher conferences, Amanda's parents were often advised that although Amanda was not overtly aggressive toward peers, she was known to be domineering and to make threats to peers seemingly to coerce them to behave as she wanted. Amanda's mother was aware of Amanda shoplifting and stealing from neighbors on a few occasions beginning at age eight. Amanda's mother later explained to the therapist that because these problem behaviors were interspersed with periods in which Amanda seemed to function adequately—she received good grades, participated in a number of extra-curricular activities, and seemed to socialize with kids her age, although she did not have a best or many close friends—Amanda's mother did not previously recognize the severity of her problem behavior. Amanda was typically passively, rather than overtly, defiant. She rarely had temper tantrums or angry outbursts, and was typically not overtly aggressive.

Amanda's mother reported that her concern about Amanda's behavior had only arisen in the last year and a half, during which time Amanda had been exhibiting retaliatory behavior. Amanda had damaged belongings of her parents when she was not permitted to do something she wanted. Amanda had brothers, ages 6 and 16, and had reportedly destroyed some of her siblings' belongings; for instance, drawing on and cutting clothing, when she was angry with them. She would usually do this unobtrusively and her brothers would later discover their destroyed belongings. Much more concerning, in the months prior to her residential treatment admission, Amanda had killed one brother's hermit crabs and thrown another brother's cat against a wall on two occasions. All of these incidents occurred when Amanda was upset with her respective sibling. Notably, Amanda seemed quiet and sneaky about these problem behaviors much of the time. They seemed planned rather than impulsive or occurring in the context of an angry outburst. When confronted with her behavior, she rarely tried to deny it, but often rationalized that the targeted person was deserving of the offense. Further, on separate occasions, Amanda had accused her older brother and a teacher of sexually abusing her. When interviewed by child protective services, on both occasions Amanda reported fabricating the allegations while feeling angry with the respective person.

Amanda initially engaged in similar conduct problems on the residential unit. Although her behavior was rarely overtly disruptive, she was found to have stolen from peers on multiple occasions and quietly defaced property. She accused both peers and staff members of inappropriately touching her at times when she was angry with these individuals. Staff was aware that she was a dominant personality on the milieu who could usually convince peers to do what she wanted. She used relational aggression and quietly bullied her peers and pitted them against one another.

Amanda's therapist recognized that Amanda seemed to align herself with her father and his relative power in the home, while she seemed to view her mother contemptuously as weak. Amanda's treatment was challenging because her parents did not work collaboratively on the presenting problems. Her father stated that he did not believe that Amanda had mental health or behavioral problems and believed Amanda should have not been admitted to the unit. Amanda's mother filed for divorce from her father during her course of residential treatment, and her father continued to remain disengaged from Amanda's treatment in spite of the therapist's ongoing attempts to engage him. It appeared to Amanda's clinical team that he was actively undermining her progress by telling Amanda that it was her mother's fault he was not living at home and that he would eventually take her to another state to live with him. However, over time, he began to have less contact with Amanda and moved out of state. Although Amanda initially struggled with the decrease in contact, she eventually began to both adapt and to show improvement on her treatment goals. During a three-week period in which Amanda's father had no contact with her, Amanda began to demonstrate steady progress. Although she continued to quietly boss her peers around and make comments intended to be hurtful both to peers who resisted her directives and staff who set limits she did not like, she began refraining from highly destructive behavior, threats to harm herself, and accusations that others hurt her. Her compliance with adult directives improved and she demonstrated some willingness and ability to handle distressing emotions in socially appropriate ways.

During this time, Amanda's mother continued to remain engaged in therapy and was able to work with Amanda on improving the child–parent relationship and communication as well as setting and maintaining clear household rules and expectations. The therapist helped Amanda's mother identify ways of talking to Amanda appropriately about her father by emphasizing that although her mother cared for him and appreciated that he and Amanda love each other, he had been making choices that were unhealthy for him and the family, which made it necessary for Amanda's mother to maintain some separation between him and the children. Amanda's mother expressed her hope to Amanda that her father would eventually choose to make healthier choices and be more present. Amanda's mother, therapist, and all involved in her care emphasized responsibility for behavioral choices, as Amanda's early exposure to the dynamics of domestic violence seemed to lead to her developing a core set of beliefs that one person can "make" another person behave a certain way by upsetting that person and that others "deserve" to be target of negative behavior when they do something that upsets another. The therapist also helped Amanda's mother identify household rules she expected Amanda to follow and clearly communicate the rules, expectations, and desired behaviors, as well as appropriate positive and negative consequences for adherence and violations, respectively.

The therapist particularly emphasized with Amanda's mother the importance of much more closely supervising Amanda in general and particularly following situations that may be upsetting for Amanda or had historically triggered negative behavior. Not only had Amanda's early experiences with domestic violence modeled aggression as a seemingly valid response to upsetting emotions, but they had created a family dynamic in which both parents were often emotionally unavailable and did not closely monitor the children. For Amanda's mother, it had been more protective to closely monitor Amanda's father rather than the children. Both Amanda's mother and all involved in Amanda's care on the milieu began to monitor Amanda's interactions with peers more closely and actively share their observations of Amanda's behavior with her in real time, praising her behavior when it was appropriate, and identifying when it was inappropriate and both modeling and coaching appropriate interactions.

Amanda and her mother had a series of successful and increasingly longer passes home during which Amanda's behavior was periodically oppositional, but never aggressive or destructive. These passes gave them an opportunity to engage in relationship building activities and practice the behavioral management strategies they had been discussing with the therapist. Amanda had always seemed to value the power her father had in the household, and this appeared to be one reason she tended to align with him. Throughout her series of passes home, Amanda appeared to start to see her mother as more empowered through her mother's efforts to stand up for the family and reorganize and run the household separate from Amanda's father. This was important because the improving relationship between Amanda and her mother was a key factor in Amanda's growing motivation to improve her conduct. Amanda did not value many things that might be used to reinforce positive behavior in other children; although she sometimes responded positively to material rewards, the response was typically very short-lived. But, she was increasingly willing to meet her mother's expectations as she came to view her mother as a more powerful person. Amanda's behavior eventually became safe and stable enough to discharge her to her mother's home.

Upon discharge from residential treatment Amanda and her family were referred to functional family therapy (FFT), which was provided twice weekly in the home. Her FFT therapists worked with Amanda and her mother to help them to understand Amanda's behavior in the context of Amanda's desire to avoid being the target of violence and rejection (similar to her mother) by valuing power and trying to establish herself as a powerful person (similar to her father). The therapists eventually helped Amanda and her mother recognize that Amanda had not been tremendously distressed by her lack of close friendships. She was more comfortable keeping peers at a distance, in order to try to avoid being hurt and rejected, and behaving in a domineering manner helped her feel safe. The therapists further worked with Amanda and her mother to identify the many ways in which Amanda learned that violence, as well as other forms of aggression and negative behavior, can be effective means of getting what one wants. Amanda's mother's growing awareness of the extent to which Amanda had been impacted by the violence in the home seemed to strengthen her resolve to avoid reconciling with Amanda's father and to only allow him access to the children when he was taking his medication consistently and demonstrating stable mood and behavior. The therapists worked toward helping Amanda learn alternative means of expressing her needs and preferences and having them met, solving problems, and tolerating negative emotions.

The therapists also worked with the whole family to help them to develop better understanding of the family relationships and dynamics in the home. They tried to address not only the present dynamics between family members, but also those that they understood were likely in effect when Amanda's father was present in the home. The therapists recognized that Amanda resented her older brother because he was protective of her mother. Amanda viewed this as a betrayal to the father she admired. Amanda also resented her younger brother who seemed to receive whatever attention Amanda's mother could spare during times Amanda's father had been unstable or abusive. Amanda's mother acknowledged that she had long tried to convince herself that Amanda was best able to care for herself among the children in the house. The therapists worked with Amanda and each of her family members in dyads and helped them to improve their respective relationships through shared activities and better communication of their feelings, needs, and preferences. Amanda and her mother in particular were encouraged to engage in shared activities to strengthen their relationship. Concurrently, Amanda's mother was encouraged to continue to maintain clear rules and behavioral expectations and apply positive and negative consequences consistently. The therapists coached Amanda's mother to help her better understand that maintaining a positive rapport with Amanda was not mutually exclusive to consistently holding Amanda accountable for her behavior. It was recommended that Amanda begin engaging in small, closely supervised extracurricular activities so she could improve her peer relations and socialization.

Amanda's conduct problems continued to show a marked decrease in intensity and frequency and FFT was discontinued. However, throughout her adolescence, Amanda's father periodically increased his contact with her or tried to gain more access to her. At times Amanda's mother was supportive of this when Amanda's father appeared more stable, but he would revert to poor self-care and with it aggressive and disruptive interactions with his family. It was during these times that Amanda's behavioral problems tended to escalate. Consequently, Amanda was re-engaged in therapy on and off throughout much of her adolescence. On two separate occasions she was arrested, once for shoplifting and once for physically attacking a peer, and both times was afforded the opportunity to participate in a diversion program through which she was required to receive therapeutic services. Fortunately, the strong therapeutic foundation that was developed during Amanda's early treatment services for both Amanda and her mother and siblings provided a reference point for later therapeutic services so that Amanda was often easy to re-engage in therapy and generally responded positively fairly readily.

Case Study 2

Louis

Louis was a 14-year-old male whose father was from the Dominican Republic. Louis' parents were 15 years old when he was born and his father returned to the Dominican Republic when Louis was an infant. Louis' mother was unable to care for him during his early years. His maternal grandmother was his primary caregiver until he was three years old, but when she developed medical problems and was no longer able to care for Louis, he was placed in foster care. When Louis was six years old, he was able to return to his mother's care. By that time, his mother had another son from a relationship with a different partner. That child's father was no longer active in his life, and Louis' mother was a single parent to both boys for about six years before a male partner moved into her home about eight months before Louis presented for therapy.

Louis was initially referred for outpatient treatment through the legal system following an adjudication for coercing a 12-year-old male cousin to perform a sex act on a 10-year-old female neighbor. Louis denied any other history of sexual misbehavior and those involved in his care knew of no other incidents; however, Louis' family did report that he frequently bullied his younger brother, cousins, and neighbor children and coerced them to misbehave. From the point of view of those who knew him, his sexual offense seemed to be part of this pattern of aggressive and other misbehavior, and his mother noted that Louis seemed to receive enjoyment from other people's humiliations as well as from eliciting angry and frustrated reactions from those around him. She imagined that Louis found the incident of the sexual behavior between the two minors that he coerced humorous and entertaining. Consistent with this description of Louis' functioning, in his early interactions with the therapist Louis had postured menacingly toward the therapist, engaged in persistent limit testing by attempting to enter the therapist's desk and filing drawers and commandeer her computer, intentionally broke items in the office, and stole from the therapist. Louis denied a history of his own sexual abuse. He related his offense to his discovery and frequent viewing of his mother's boyfriend's collection of pornography, as well as later discovering and frequently viewing pornography on the Internet via the family's home computer, cell phones, and gaming devices. He had stolen others' cell phones and gaming devices on multiple occasions and used them to view pornography. He described the incident of sexual behavior he coerced between the two other minors as "just playing around," and "funny," and indicated he did not understand why others were so upset about it.

Louis' mother described Louis as "spoiled" during the years she was a single parent to him and his brother who was five years younger than Louis. She acknowledged that she set few limits with Louis, in part because she felt guilty about the years she and Louis were separated, and often gave in to his demands or overlooked negative behavior. At other times, she overreacted out of a sense of frustration. For instance, she would attempt to ground Louis for months at a time or "cancel" Christmas by withholding all gifts and other celebratory activities related to the holiday. Louis' mother also acknowledged that for a few years after Louis returned to her care, she spent a lot of time out partying with friends and males she was casually dating. She often left Louis and his brother in the care of whoever was willing to watch them for an evening, sometimes with people with whom she was not very familiar. When she was home with her sons, her friends and acquaintances were often hanging out in her home drinking and smoking marijuana. By the time Louis presented for therapy, his mother reported that she had stopped partying and using substances a few years back. However, although the family denied when specifically asked, there seemed to be multiple factors that suggested that Louis' mother's boyfriend may have brought drug activity back into the home, as well as the chaos of multiple people of limited familiarity coming and going in the home.

In the couple of years prior to Louis' offense, his mother was aware that his behavior was increasingly problematic. His teachers described him as a "bully," and he was frequently aggressive toward his peers and his brother. More recently, he had also become threatening and menacing towards adults. Louis stole frequently from both people and stores. He had recently started stealing others' credit cards and ordering merchandise online. He intentionally broke others' belongings, especially his brother's belongings. He stayed out with his friends long past the time he was expected home and had left home a few times without permission. Recently, he had also started leaving school during the day and was failing most of his classes. Louis' mother acknowledged that her efforts to address Louis' behavior were generally short-lived because "he just wears me down and does what he wants anyway."

Louis' mother had started dating her boyfriend less than a year before the start of Louis' therapy. The relationship had quickly progressed and her boyfriend moved into the family's home. At the start of Louis' therapy, his mother indicated that she expected that her boyfriend would effectively discipline Louis and remedy his conduct problems. She expected Louis to respond more readily to a male authority figure and had ceded responsibility for Louis' discipline to her boyfriend. Louis' mom stated that Louis would have to "get used to the fact that he is not the man of the house anymore." Although Louis' mother's boyfriend did not attend Louis' initial outpatient therapy sessions in spite of the therapist's urging, it appeared to the therapist that Louis continued to feel like his mother's boyfriend was a near stranger living in his home, one who periodically yelled at him and made similar punitive threats to Louis' mother, but rarely followed through. Although Louis and his mother denied at the start of therapy that mother's boyfriend ever physically punished Louis, Louis indicated that his mother's boyfriend was physically intimidating and reported that he "gets in my face" while yelling and threatening physical punishment, which Louis' mother also acknowledged.

Unfortunately, in the early weeks of outpatient therapy, Louis' mother's reliance on her boyfriend to provide discipline seemed to lead to an increase in Louis' anger and behavior problems. Louis began leaving the home and staying out without permission more often. When his mother and her boyfriend more actively tried to prevent him from leaving, he became aggressive toward them. His mother's boyfriend responded with more aggression, which required the therapist to make a number of reports to child protective services. These were briefly investigated and closed with the stipulation that Louis and his family continue therapy. Although Louis was initially referred for office-based outpatient therapy to address his sexual offending, the therapist recommended home-based multisystemic therapy (MST).

Providing MST in Louis' home, community, and school provided a more intensive level of service more appropriate for the severity of his conduct problems. The therapy team was also hopeful that it would increase the engagement of Louis' mother and her boyfriend by having the therapists go to them at days and times they reported were most convenient. This seemed to effectively reduce the attendance barrier for Louis' mother, who had missed some early outpatient therapy sessions after obtaining a new job at a fast-food establishment that required variable shifts. The home and community-based treatment modality was a moderately effective approach at engaging Louis' mother's boyfriend who reluctantly agreed to participate in services, but would still be absent from the home for about half the sessions scheduled at his reported convenience.

The therapist attempted to have both Louis and the adults in the home identify desired behaviors and other goals for Louis. Louis' mother and boyfriend initially struggled with this. They were initially able to identify only that they wanted Louis to avoid behaviors that resulted in legal system involvement, calls from school, and complaints from neighbors. The therapy team noted both that there was a tendency to overlook certain behaviors until the behavior somehow resulted in inconvenience for the adults. For instance, bullying and viewing pornography had not been addressed as a problem with Louis until the former resulted in complaints from neighbors and the school and until the latter was associated with Louis' sexual offense. The adults also seemed to have difficulty identifying the positive behaviors or goals they would like to see from Louis and it seemed to the therapy team that perhaps the adults in Louis' life had not considered a positive life trajectory for him other than trying to stay out of trouble. Once the adults in the home were able to identify some positive behaviors they hoped to see from Louis, the therapy team attempted to work with them on understanding the primary ways in which behaviors are learned and reinforced and especially encouraged modeling the types of behavior they expected from Louis; however, a noteworthy challenge and frequent theme to the treatment process was that Louis' mother and her boyfriend stated their belief that as adults of the home they were entitled to behave differently than the children in the home. The therapy team also tried to work with Louis' mother and her boyfriend to learn effective behavior management strategies and to utilize them consistently, although throughout much of treatment Louis' mother continued to report attempting to institute excessively long or severe consequences for behavior. The therapy team endeavored to help her and her boyfriend recognize that these lengthy and severe consequences had very limited impact because they occurred too infrequently, allowed limited, if any, opportunity for Louis to receive reinforcement for a return to acceptable behavior, and were generally associated with poor follow-through.

Louis also initially had difficulty identifying goals for himself other than to "get off probation." The therapy team engaged him by making this a primary treatment goal and offering to help him make progress toward this goal desired outcome. The team used a cognitive behavioral approach to help Louis identify the ways he had learned the behaviors that were causing him problems, including the sexually inappropriate behavior that led to his therapy referral, as well as to identify both environmental and internal triggers to these behaviors, including examining automatic thoughts and beliefs. The team continued to work with Louis to identify other factors that might motivate him to progress in therapy in addition to completing his probationary requirements. Louis eventually identified that he would like a means to earn money. He had been spending a lot of unsupervised time with older individuals in the neighborhood, and his therapy team was concerned that he may have started to get involved in drug distribution. The team worked with Louis to help him apply for jobs, practice interview skills, and prepare to meet the expectations of an employer. Louis eventually obtained employment at a different franchise of the same fast-food establishment as his mother. In addition to the sense of responsibility and appropriate independence the job seemed to bring Louis, it also gave him and his mother common ground around which to communicate and seemed to have a positive impact on their relationship.

During the therapy team's work with Louis at his school, they did notice that there were a couple of male staff members to whom Louis seemed to respond positively. The team was able to work with Louis to identify what about these individuals he respected and responded well to. Louis' feedback in conjunction with the therapy team's observations enabled them to provide recommendations to school staff regarding alternative ways of helping Louis manage his behavior. The therapy team was also able to engage one of Louis' preferred school staff members to become more involved with Louis during the school day and serve in the role of a mentor. This seemed to reduce Louis' truancy and incidents of physical altercations at school. Verbal bullying remained a problem that the therapy team continued to address. This staff member encouraged Louis to participate in a club the staff member supervised after school. Although Louis' interest in and commitment to this activity was variable, he did attend occasionally, which gave him some exposure to peers who were engaged in positive activities and in conjunction with his job, reduced the amount of unstructured time he had been using previously to hang out with older males in the neighborhood who his team suspected were engaging him in criminal behavior.

Louis made moderate progress. He demonstrated a significant reduction in major behavioral violations, including aggression, stealing, being out of the home without permission, and stealing. There were no more known incidents of sexually inappropriate or offensive behavior, although his mother was aware that he continued to access pornography periodically. Louis continued to have a tendency to antagonize his brother, cousins, and peers and continued to seem to experience some satisfaction in this. The family conflict decreased when Louis started avoiding behaviors that caused his mother and her boyfriend the inconvenience of others complaining about Louis' behavior, and the reduction in conflict was associated with a reduction in Louis' anger. The major barrier to a good prognosis for Louis was that his mother and her boyfriend continued to struggle to modify their approaches to parenting and behavior management, a stance that was ironically reinforced from their viewpoint by the behavioral improvements Louis was otherwise demonstrating. The therapists were hopeful that Louis' growing independence and time away from his family involved in positive activities would help sustain some of the changes he had made and offer him alternative possibilities for his future, but were realistic that without parenting and household changes, it would not be unexpected for Louis to revert to some of his previous problem behaviors.

Case Study 3
David

David was a four-year-old boy who first presented for therapy with his mother shortly after she had fled from her marriage with David's father and moved with David and his two-year-old sister many states away to live with her aunt. David's mother reported that David's father was regularly severely abusive toward her. She reported that David's father had been occasionally physically abusive to the children as well. Child protective services had become involved in their home state and insisted that David's father live separately from the children and have no unsupervised contact. According to David's mother, David's father blamed her for this circumstance and began stalking her at her place of employment. She feared for her life and saw no other means of protecting herself and her children, but to flee.

David's mom arrived to her aunt's home with no money, job, or resources and David's behavior was placing the family's living situation with the aunt in jeopardy. David seemed to refuse almost all adult directives, often screaming forcefully when given instructions or directions. He threw long, loud, and sometimes violent temper tantrums during which he sometimes hurt himself by banging his head. He frequently ran from his mother in public and ran out of the house on multiple occasions into the busy street on which the house was situated. David exhibited tremendous hyperactivity, rarely sitting still for more than a minute or two before running around with abandon. His sleep was poor so his mother rarely had an opportunity to rest or relax. He destroyed most of his belongings and was aggressive toward his younger sister, on one occasion causing substantial injury to her eye. David's behaviors were consistent with criteria for both ODD and ADHD; however, his treatment team was aware that his presenting problems were probably rooted at least to some extent in posttraumatic stress due to the ongoing violence he had experienced and witnessed in his home.

David was referred for parent–child interaction therapy (PCIT). However, his behavior was initially so dysregulated that the therapist could not safely provide PCIT in the home nor could his mother safely transport David for office-based sessions. David was then referred to a partial hospitalization program where he was able to receive more intensive psychiatric treatment. Although David's mother expressed some reluctance given David's age, she agreed to the conservative use of a stimulant medication, which helped to alleviate some of David's hyperactivity and impulsivity, and to the use of melatonin to improve sleep. At the urging of a care coordination team with which David became linked, the PCIT provider agreed to resume PCIT in the partial hospital setting at the end of the treatment day so that David could remain in a safe setting during initial sessions.

David's mother had spent most of David's life herself in a state of heightened arousal due to the abuse she was experiencing in her marriage, and she acknowledged using harsh parenting practices in an effort to try to gain compliance from David in order to try to avoid incidents of his father physically hurting him when he misbehaved. Consequently, David and his mother never had the opportunity to develop a strong and positive attachment to one another. The PCIT treatment protocol focuses on first strengthening the parent–child bond, as the secure attachment and strong relationship between the parent and child is viewed as the foundation to effective parenting and discipline. In the safety of the partial hospitalization program, David's mother was eventually able to relax around David sufficiently to begin engaging with him in his love of toy cars and trains. The child-directed interaction phase of PCIT enables the parent to learn to play with their child in a way that enhances the parent–child bond. During this phase of treatment, David's mother began designating special play time with David and his sister in the evenings as well and practicing the skills she was learning in PCIT in the home. David's aunt, who initially declined to participate in treatment, noticed the early positive changes in both David and his mother, and began attending treatment sessions as well and learning the skills associated with PCIT.

The second phase of PCIT, Parent-Directed Interaction, started just before David's discharge from the partial hospitalization program and continued in an office-based setting two days per week. This setting allowed for the therapist to observe interactions between David and his caregivers through a one-way mirror and offer directions through a bud-in-the-ear mechanism. During this phase of treatment, David's mother and aunt learned how to issue clear and developmentally appropriate directives to David, how to offer meaningful praise for compliance to reinforce this desired behavior, and how to apply a brief, meaningful, and developmentally appropriate consequence for noncompliance. The therapist used a coding system to offer feedback to David's caregivers and assigned practice between sessions. In fact, David's mother and aunt began to code each other's interactions with David in the home and were remarkably open to one another's feedback! They both noted that the skills they were learning were equally effective with David's younger sister.

The therapist discussed with David's mother and aunt the importance of the stable and predictable home life they were creating for David and his sister as a major therapeutic factor complementing the formal therapy David was receiving. They discussed routines related to meals, bedtimes, and other transitional periods during the day, as well as balancing activities such as active play, quiet play, and structured and unstructured time. Treatment also focused on helping David and his caregivers learn easy self-soothing techniques that David's mother could offer when she noticed him becoming emotionally overwhelmed. During the course of PCIT, David's mother worked with his care coordinator to seek approval for David to enter a therapeutic nursery school where there was a low staff-to-student ratio and staff with formal mental health training who were able to respond effectively to David's behavioral health challenges. David thrived in that environment and by the end of the nursery school year, his mother, treatment team, and educational team all thought it was appropriate for him to start kindergarten in a regular educational setting. With the support of her aunt, David's mother was eventually able to complete her nursing education she had started before her marriage and obtain gainful employment and her own residence near the aunt, who remained a supporter and resource. David and his mother periodically continued to stop in to visit his therapist, and reportedly continued to maintain their progress following formal cessation of treatment.

Case Study 4

Jane

Jane was a 12-year-old girl of African American descent. She had been admitted to residential treatment after attempting to disconnect the breathing machine of her foster parent's mother. Jane had been placed into foster care after her mother, who was her primary caregiver, had relapsed into drug use. Jane's parents had been separated from an early age. Her father was significantly older than her mother and lived in a different state. Jane did not have much contact with her father. Jane was in a regular education setting prior to her admission to residential treatment and did not have an Individualized Education Program or receive any learning or behavioral supports at school or at home. She attended an under-resourced and low-achieving school in a neighborhood with a high crime rate. Upon intake, her mother reported that in response to being teased one day after school, Jane threw a brick in the face of a peer, severely injuring him. Jane had also poured bleach into a fish tank previously. Jane's mother had regained her sobriety and Jane's goal upon discharge from the residential setting would be to return to the care of her mother. Jane's maternal grandmother was also involved with her and her family.

When asked during treatment why she had attempted to disconnect the breathing machine of her foster grandmother, Jane answered "I just wanted her to stop talking" and could not identify any further motivation beyond that. In treatment, Jane was able to do very well behaviorally, often earning most of her points in the behavior modification system. She very rarely engaged in any aggressive or otherwise problematic behaviors with her peers or with staff while in treatment. She was noted by her therapist to become very emotionally overwrought when upset in a way that was not typical of most children her age, once stating to her therapist "everything was going great until you came along!" She also became upset when she perceived being embarrassed in any way. While in treatment, she participated in a group targeting bullying among peers. She did an excellent job in the group and demonstrated correct answers to every question. Once in the anti-bullying group, a direct care staff member who was present made a comment about Jane being a bully in front of the entire group. Jane became visibly upset and walked out. Afterwards, Jane's group therapist explained to the staff member that despite what might be a perceived as a tough exterior, Jane likely felt shamed and humiliated in that moment. The staff member later apologized to Jane, which Jane seemed to appreciate.

Jane's mother, who had successfully regained her sobriety while Jane was in foster care, was sporadically involved in treatment and as more was learned about their family, it appeared that Jane had been parentified during periods when her mother relapsed and had acted as a parent to her mother during some of these periods. One particular story involved Jane physically barring her mother's access to drugs, a time that Jane was able to recall as a terrifying and distressing experience. Jane's mother also displayed some symptoms of a possible personality disorder. Therapy with Jane and her mother focused on re-structuring the roles of parent and child, and allowing Jane to process some of the difficult times she had been through with her mother, which included a great deal of anxiety, shame, and fear on Jane's part. Jane also processed many of these thoughts and feelings in individual therapy using a blend of trauma-focused cognitive behavioral therapy and psychoeducation. Toward the end of her time in treatment, which was relatively short given her ability to do well in the behavior modification system and therapeutic milieu, her therapist worked in family sessions on safety planning in the future so that Jane and her mother could discuss how they could each handle potential problems should they arise around her mother's relapse, possible domestic violence in the home, or other safety issues. Jane's mother also worked with the school district staff both in the facility and from her local district to get her into a new school where her grandmother had worked; the new school was a better regarded school for its resources and achievement. She was successfully discharged to her mother with a new school to attend. Family-based support services to help her and her mother maintain their gains and prevent another out-of-home placement for Jane were also implemented.

Case Study 5

Michael

Michael was a seven-year-old boy of Puerto Rican and Italian descent. He was referred by child protective services with a request to be seen as soon as possible for safety concerns. Michael's primary caregiver was his mother; he had not had contact with his father since the time he was about one or two years old. While living with his mother and younger sister and brother, he had apparently entered his younger sister's room one night and anally penetrated her. There was no known history of Michael being a victim of child sexual abuse himself. He had also killed the family cat, and set fires in the home within the same year. Michael also struggled behaviorally and academically at school and was receiving behavioral support services in school. Michael's mother lived in a neighborhood where violence was frequent and his local school was performing so poorly that it had nearly been closed by the school district on at least one occasion. In school, Michael was also reported to have poor boundaries with other children. Michael easily met criteria for conduct disorder, childhood onset. Michael also carried a diagnosis of ADHD and at some point had begun seeing a psychiatrist who prescribed him stimulant medication.

Michael's impulsivity and poor understanding of boundaries seemed to be exacerbated by the instability in his life. His grandmother and her various paramours were actively using drugs, and there appeared to be many strangers in and out of the house both for his grandparents and for his mother, who also had experienced housing instability. Michael's mother had three children and cared for them on her own while also caring for her drug addicted mother and managing her own bipolar depression and physical health issues brought on by obesity. After Michael was removed from her home, his mother had a fourth child with a man who was arrested and jailed while the baby was in utero.

Following the sexual misbehavior towards his sister which prompted the evaluation referral, child protective services had too much difficulty finding an appropriate foster home for Michael and so the decision was made to leave Michael in the care of his mother and remove the two younger children from the home and place them into a foster home. When Michael was first evaluated, there were no other children in the home and he was receiving in home social services visits twice a week, but there were still concerns about supervision and safety. The safety recommendations for Michael included having him in "line of sight" supervision such that he was always in the sight of an adult when at school or at home and awake. They also included no access to combustibles or to pets.

In the evaluation, Michael's mother described that when she was out of the home, she left him in the care of her own mother who was actively using crack cocaine. During one of the times that Michael's grandmother was watching him, an in-home services worker was there as part of a regularly planned visit and discovered that Michael was able to set a small fire using the stove burner. In the incident where Michael killed a pet cat, it appeared that his mother had asked him to get the cat out from under a wardrobe, which he did using an instrument. In trying to swat the cat out from under the bureau and left to his own devices, he accidentally killed their family pet.

There were also concerns with Michael's mother's use of corporal punishment, and child protective services had been called at least twice after Michael reported being beaten, at least once with a broom handle, by his mother. After Michael's initial evaluation for both treatment and safety, it appeared that despite his young age and the multiple precautions put into place, it was still unsafe for Michael to be in the home. He appeared to be both at risk to himself and to others in the household. He also appeared to be at risk for more potential physical abuse. The decision to have his siblings removed when one was abused by Michael, and have Michael remain in the home, also complicated the recovery of his sister and added complicated dynamics and guilt to the relationship between him and his family. Immediately following the evaluation, his evaluator convened a conference call with the referral source at child protective services and Michael's managed care company to discuss possible out-of-home placements, such as a residential treatment facility. Given his young age, no facility was appropriate, and the plan was to try to place Michael in a therapeutic foster home as soon as an appropriate one became available. He was soon placed in a therapeutic foster home. Michael began treatment with his mother shortly after being referred, despite not living at home anymore. Both his mother and his foster parent would attend outpatient therapy targeting his sexualized and aggressive behaviors as part of adjunctive treatment. Therapy began with common and age-appropriate CBT components, such as teaching about the identification of emotions, while building rapport. Because of the acuity of the safety issues involved with Michael, there was a strong early emphasis on psychoeducation around appropriate boundaries and body safety. During the course of treatment it came out that Michael and his siblings had witnessed his mother engaged in anal sex with her paramour at least once if not multiple times. The therapist also noted that Michael's mother openly spoke about inappropriately explicit topics, usually of a sexual nature, in front of him, and worked with her on increasing her awareness of this and being mindful of not discussing inappropriate details of adult sexuality with or in front of Michael. His therapist also reviewed his safety plan with his foster parent in every session to ensure that the guidelines were being followed and to see if any adjustments needed to be made.

This included components such as teaching about personal space, and practicing identifying "OK" and "Not OK" touches with Michael in session, then sharing this in individual and joint sessions with Michael's caregivers. Anger management, including identifying and practicing emotional regulation techniques, was practiced in session with the use of a child-friendly visual "emotions thermometer" which could act as a measure of Subjective Units of Distress for a child to identify emotional intensity.

In treatment individually, Michael was sweet, engaging, and responded well to various activities. With his mother, Michael appeared to take a role that was more of a caregiver than would be expected for a child his age. Although he moved a few times for reasons unrelated to his behavior, which caused him to miss school due to transferring to different schools, he eventually did find a placement in the same city where he could attend a nearby school that appeared to be better organized and less riddled with structural problems than his previous school where his mother lived.

Michael appeared to benefit from the stability and support received from the foster family that he ended up staying with the longest. In treatment, he also did very well continuing with the CBT-based curriculum for sexual behavior problems that culminated in him writing an apology letter to his younger sister. Michael's biological mother also participated in therapy with him and later with him and his sister as much as possible.

In individual sessions with Michael's therapist, his mother described her own history of childhood trauma, which was marked by the drug addiction that compromised the abilities of both of her parents. Michael's mother described that she herself was in and out of foster care and had been sexually and emotionally abused while in some of these homes. The times when she was in the care of her mother, she was often parentified as the oldest child, and had to find ways to support her siblings and her mother's addiction; sometimes this included engaging in prostitution while still a child. Michael's mother began to also see her own therapist to address her past history and untreated trauma. While she loved her children dearly, she had never had a model of appropriate and stable parenting on which to base her own parenting practice of her four children. As an adult, Michael's mother continued to struggle with caring for her own mother, who still struggled with an addiction to crack cocaine and who relied upon Michael's mother for housing and money. Limit setting and substance abuse services for Michael's grandmother were addressed in sessions; child protective services also made his grandmother's leaving the home a condition of allowing Michael and his siblings back into their mother's home.

Eventually, his younger sister started her own trauma treatment and her therapist and Michael's coordinated with one another so that the siblings could start having limited contact in therapy in order to build on the gains they had both made and work toward possible future reunification. Eventually, Michael was able to share his apology letter (which had been shared beforehand with everyone involved) with his sister in person in therapy. The younger siblings had been reunited with their mother after Michael was removed from the home. Michael was eventually permitted to have supervised visits with his mother and siblings at home. These went well until it was reported that Michael was with his siblings on a walk to a store without adult supervision, and then the visits were paused.

Michael continued to progress in his own treatment; however, his mother had additional struggles of her own, including incarceration after she brought drugs to her paramour in jail. Michael was able to stay with his foster family while this occurred, and while he missed his mother and his previous visits with her, he grew closer with his foster mother and appeared to benefit from the routine, stability, and consistency that her household provided. Visits with his biological siblings, who were placed at different foster homes, became more difficult and Michael went through a long period of having no contact again with his sister with whom he had successfully started the reunification process.

Despite carrying a diagnosis of ADHD, he had never received a psychoeducational evaluation and Michael continued to struggle in school. A closer analysis of his behavior in school revealed that much of his misbehavior seemed to be around tests and avoiding other academic work. His therapist worked with his family and treatment team to request a psychoeducational evaluation through his school in order to best iden-tify and address his learning and academic issues, which would likely lead to a reduction in his need to escape instruction situations by misbehaving.

Eventually, after Michael had completed all of the reunification work he could do while he, his sister, and his mother were no longer in regular contact, and had no longer required the same level of supervision around his behavior, he was successfully discharged from outpatient treatment. He had not displayed any problematic sexual behaviors in over a year, and had not attempted any sexual behaviors as severe as the incident that brought him into treatment since that incident occurred. He also had not attempted to engage in any firesetting or animal cruelty, and in fact, was able to live in a household with a small dog. At the time of his discharge, his mother remained incarcerated and so he remained with the foster family he had been living with, while his siblings were in different foster homes. Michael still received supports through school-based therapeutic staff, his foster parent, and a therapist from his foster agency. Upon dis-charge from the sexual behavior specific therapy, the recommendation was made for Michael and his sister to re-engage in treatment together should reunification toward living in the same home be attempted in the future.

Conclusion

Disruptive Behavior Disorders account for a larger portion of public health expenditures than do chronic childhood illnesses (Guevara, Mandell, Rostain, Zhao, & Hadley, 2003). When left untreated, they can result in a host of negative outcomes for youth, such as delinquency, dropping out of school, teen pregnancy, and substance abuse problems. These problems can also lead to negative trajectories for the adults that these youth will one day become, at great cost to the individual and their families, as well as to society. In addition to the financial and emotional costs, there is also a cost to the potential of our society when children who could be contributing their skills, their ideas, their creativity, their hopes, and their other talents as they grow into young adults end up on a pathway where they will not be able to develop and contribute those talents.

When we consider the fact that many children diagnosed with disruptive behavior disorders are coming from marginalized families in underserved communities with under-resourced schools, preventing and treating these disorders becomes an imperative for clinicians, citizens, and policy-makers alike. Effective treatments exist to help treat disruptive behavior problems. While there cannot be a one-size-fits-all approach to treating these behavior problems, there are now more resources available to find and select an approach that will be evidence based, and even more efforts to identify and disseminate effective best practice.

In order to best treat a disruptive behavior disorder in a child or adolescent, it is essential to understand that child or adolescent and identify the internal and external forces at work behind their problematic behaviors. It is also essential to understand the meaning of that child's behavior in the context of their daily life and environment. For most youth, the most effective treatment will also include the involvement of caregivers and coordination or even involvement with other systems in the child's life, such as school and community.

While there is an increased risk of developing more chronic and severe behavior problems when diagnosed with conduct disorder, childhood onset, we also know that none of these diagnoses now constitute a "life sentence" with proper identification, treatment, and support. Human beings, especially children, have an amazing capacity for successful adaptation in the face of adversity, a construct that is often referred to as resilience. We can also prevent the development of more serious problems in youth by capitalizing on this capacity and increasing the factors which we know can help protect children from negative outcomes, such as more effective schooling, and more effective and positive parenting and discipline practices. It has become increasingly useful to view many of the children referred for disruptive behaviors and defiance by asking "What happened to you?" instead of "What's wrong with you?" Addressing untreated trauma through the increasingly widespread use of trauma-informed care in schools and in clinical settings will also contribute to prevention and early detection of behavior problems, as will reducing ineffective and overly punitive discipline in these settings. A continued focus on effective intervention and prevention for these disorders can hopefully reduce their prevalence and severity, improving life for the children and families who are most at risk.

References

Adams, C. J. (2015). Trends in high school dropout and completion rates in the United States: 1972–2012. *Education Week, 34*(36).

Are zero tolerance policies effective in the schools? An evidentiary review and recommendations. (2008). *American Psychologist, 63*(9), 852–862. doi:10.1037/0003-066X.63.9.852

American Psychiatric Association. (1952). *Diagnostic and statistical manual of mental disorders* (1st ed.). Washington, DC: Author.

American Psychiatric Association. (1980) *Diagnostic and statistical manual of mental disorders* (3rd ed.). Washington, DC: Author.

American Psychiatric Association. (1994). *Diagnostic and statistical manual of mental disorders* (4th ed.). Washington, DC: Author.

American Psychiatric Association. (2000). *Diagnostic and statistical manual of mental disorders* (4th ed., Text Rev.). Washington, DC: Author.

American Psychiatric Association. (2013a). *Diagnostic and statistical manual of mental disorders* (5th ed.). Washington, DC: Author.

American Psychiatric Association. (2013b). *Highlights of changes from DSM-IV-TR to DSM-5*. Retrieved from www.dsm5.org/documents/changes%20from%20 dsm-iv-tr%20to%20dsm-5.pdf

American Psychological Association. (2012). *Facing the school dropout dilemma*. Washington, DC: Author. Retrieved from www.apa.org/pi/families/resources /school-dropout-prevention.aspx

Barnao, M., Ward, T., & Robertson, P. (2016). The good lives model: A new paradigm for forensic mental health. *Psychiatry, Psychology and Law, 23*(2), 288–301. doi:10.1080/13218719.2015.1054923

Battagliese, G., Caccetta, M., Luppino, O. I., Baglioni, C., Cardi, V., Mancini, F., & Buonanno, C. (2015). Cognitive-behavioral therapy for externalizing disorders: A meta-analysis of treatment effectiveness. *Behaviour Research & Therapy, 75,* 60–71. doi:10.1016/j.brat.2015.10.008

Baumrind, D. (1966). Effects of authoritative control on child behavior. *Child Development, 37,* 887–907.

Berkowski, M., & MacDonald, D. A. (2014). Childhood trauma and the development of paranormal beliefs. *Journal of Nervous and Mental Disease, 202*(4), 305–312. doi:10.1097/NMD.0000000000000123

Blair, R. J. R. (2013). The neurobiology of psychopathic traits in youths. *Nature Reviews: Neuroscience, 14,* 786–799.

Borum, R., Bartel, P., & Forth, A. (2003). *Manual for the structured assessment of violence risk in youth, Version 1.1.* Tampa: University of South Florida.

Bronfenbrenner, U. (1977). Toward an experimental ecology of human development. *American Psychologist, 32*(7), 513–531. doi:10.1037/0003-066X.32.7.513

Brown, L. (2008). *Cultural competence in trauma therapy: Beyond the Flashback.* Washington, DC: American Psychological Association.

Burke, J. D., Loeber, R., & Lahey, B. B. (2003). Course and outcomes. In C. A. Essau (Ed.), *Conduct and oppositional defiant disorders: Epidemiology, risk factors, and treatment* (pp. 61–94). Mahwah, NJ: Lawrence Erlbaum Associates Publishers.

Cadoret, R. J., Yates, W. R., Ed, T., Woodworth, G., & Stewart, M.A. (1995). Genetic-environmental interaction in the genesis of aggressivity and conduct disorders. *Archives of General Psychiatry, 52*(11), 916–924.

Canino, G., Polanczyk, G., Bauermeister, J. J., Rohde, L. A., & Frick, P. J. (2010). Does the prevalence of CD and ODD vary across cultures? *Social Psychiatry and Psychiatric Epidemiology, 45*(7), 695–704. doi:10.1007/s00127-010-0242-y

Chaffin, M., Hanson, R., Saunders, B. E., Nichols, T., Barnett, D., Zeanah, C., . . . Miller-Perrin, C. (2006). Report of the APSAC Task Force on Attachment Therapy, Reactive Attachment Disorder, and Attachment Problems. *Child Maltreatment, 11*(1), 76–89. doi:10.1177/1077559505283699

Cohen, J., Mannarino, A. P., & Deblinger, E. (2006). *Treating trauma and traumatic grief in children and adolescents.* New York, NY: The Guilford Press.

Colalillo, S., & Johnston, C. (2016). Parenting cognition and affective outcomes following parent management training: a systematic review. *Clinical Child & Family Psychology Review, 19*(3), 216–235. doi:10.1007/s10567-016-0208-z

Costello, E. J., Compton, S. N., Keeler, G., & Angold, A. (2003). Relationships between poverty and psychopathology: A natural experiment. *JAMA: Journal of the American Medical Association, 290*(15), 2023–2029.

Dannon, P. N., Aizer, A., & Lowengrub, K. (2006). Kleptomania: Differential diagnosis and treatment modalities. *Current Psychiatry Reviews, 2*(2), 281–283. doi:10.2174/157340006776875996

Darnell, A. J., & Schuler, M. S. (2015). Quasi-experimental study of functional family therapy effectiveness for juvenile justice aftercare in a racially and ethnically diverse community sample. *Children and Youth Services Review, 50,* 75–82. doi:10.1016/j.childyouth.2015.01.013

DeVore, D. W. (2011). Functional family therapy and multisystemic therapy: Doing more with less. *Corrections Today, 73*(1), 20–23.

Diehle, J., Opmeer, B. C., Boer, F., Mannarino, A. P., & Lindauer, R. L. (2015). Trauma-focused cognitive behavioral therapy or eye movement desensitization and reprocessing: What works in children with posttraumatic stress symptoms? A randomized controlled trial. *European Child & Adolescent Psychiatry, 24*(2), 227–236. doi:10.1007/s00787-014-0572-5

Dodge, K. A., & Pettit, G. S. (2003). A biopsychosocial model of the development of chronic conduct problems in adolescence. *Developmental Psychology, 39*(2), 349–371.

Epperson, D. L., Ralston, C. A., Fowers, D., & DeWitt, J. (2005). *Development of a sexual offense recidivism risk assessment tool—II (JSORRAT-II).* Unpublished manuscript, University of Iowa, Ames.

Fairchild, G., Hagan, C. C., Walsh, N. D., Passamonti, L, Calder, A. J., & Goodyer, I. M. (2013). Brain structure abnormalities in adolescent girls with conduct disorder. *Journal of Child Psychiatry, 54*(1), 86–95.

Finger, E. C., Marsh, A. A., Blair, K. S., Reid, M. E., Sims, C., Ng, P., . . . Blair, R. J. R. (2011). Disrupted reinforcement signaling in the orbitofrontal cortex and caudate in youth with conduct disorder or oppositional defiant disorder and a high level of psychopathic traits. *American Journal of Psychiatry, 168*(2), 152–162.

Foa, E., Chrestman, K. R., & Gilboa-Schechtman, E. (2009). *Prolonged exposure therapy for adolescents with PTSD: Emotional processing of traumatic experiences.* New York, NY: Oxford University Press.

Forth, A., Kosson, D., & Hare, R. D. (2003). *Hare Psychopathy Checklist: Youth Version.* Multi-Health Systems.

Frick, P. J. (2016). Current research on conduct disorder in children and adolescents. *South African Journal of Psychology, 46*(2), 160–174. doi:10.1177 /0081246316628455 sap.sagepub.com

Frick, P. J., Ray, V. J., Thornton, L. C., & Kahn, R. E. (2014a). Annual research review: A developmental psychopathology approach to understanding callous-unemotional traits in children and adolescents with serious conduct problems. *Journal of Child Psychology and Psychiatry, 55*(6), 532–548.

Frick, P. J., Ray, J. V., Thornton, L. C., & Kahn, R. E. (2014b). Can callous-unemotional traits enhance the understanding, diagnosis, and treatment of serious conduct problems in children and adolescents? A comprehensive review. *Psychological Bulletin, 140*(1), 1–57.

Gacono, C. B., & Hughes, T. L. (2004). Differentiating emotional disturbance from social maladjustment: Assessing psychopathy in aggressive youth. *Psychology in the Schools, 41*(8), 849–860. doi:10.1002/pits.20041

Garbarino, J. (2015). *Listening to killers: Lessons learned from my twenty years as a psychological expert witness in murder cases.* Oakland: University of California Press.

Garcia-Amador, M., Merchán-Naranjo, J., Tapia, C., Moreno, C., Castro-Fornieles, J., Baeza, I., . . . Arango, C. (2015). Neurological adverse effects of antipsychotics in children and adolescents. *Journal Of Clinical Psychopharmacology, 35*(6), 686–693. doi:10.1097/JCP.0000000000000419

Gifford-Smith, M., Dodge, K. A., Dishion, T. J., & McCord, J. (2005). Peer Influence in Children and adolescents: Crossing the bridge from developmental to intervention science. *Journal of Abnormal Child Psychology, 33*(3), 255–265. doi:10.1007/s10802-005-3563-7

Gilpin, A. T., Brown, M. M., & Pierucci, J. M. (2015) Relations between fantasy orientation and emotion regulation in preschool. *Early Education and Development, 26*(7), 920–932. doi:10.1080/10409289.2015.1000716

Grant, J. E., & Kim, S. W. (2002). Adolescent kleptomania treated with naltrexone: A case report. *European Child & Adolescent Psychiatry, 11*(2), 92–95. doi:10.1007/s007870200016

Green-Hennessy, S., & Hennessy, K. D. (2015). Predictors of seclusion or restraint use within residential treatment centers for children and adolescents. *Psychiatric Quarterly, 86*(4), 545–554. doi:10.1007/s11126-015-9352-8

Guevara, J. P., Mandell, D. S., Rostain, A. L., Zhao, H., & Hadley, T. R. (2003). Disparities in the reporting and treatment of health conditions in children: An analysis of the Medical Expenditure Panel Survey. *Health Services Research, 41*(2), 532–549. doi:10.1111/j.1475-6773.2005.00484.x

Hare, R. D. (1993). *Without conscience: The disturbing world of psychopaths among us.* New York, NY: The Guilford Press.

Hempel, I., Buck, N., Cima, M., & van Marle, H. (2013). Review of risk assessment instruments for juvenile sex offenders: What is next? *International Journal of Offender Therapy and Comparative Criminology, 57*(2), 208–228. doi:10.1177/0306624X11428315

Hemphala, M., & Hodgins, S. (2014). Do psychopathic traits assessed in mid-adolescence predict mental health, psychosocial, and antisocial, including criminal outcomes, over the subsequent 5 years? *Canadian Journal of Psychiatry, 59*(1), 40–49.

Hicks, B. M., Krueger, R. F., Iacono, W. G., McGue, M., & Patrick, C.J. (2004). Family transmission and heritability of externalizing disorders: A twin-family study. *Archives of General Psychiatry, 61*(9), 922–928.

Hosp, J. L., & Reschly, D. J. (2002). Predictors of restrictiveness of placement for African American and Caucasian students. *Exceptional Children, 68*(2), 225.

Hurley, N., Guckenberg, S., Persson, H., Fronius, T., & Petrosino, A. (2015, June). *What further research is needed on restorative justice in schools?* San Francisco, CA: West Ed.

Ipser, J., & Stein, D. J. (2007). Systematic review of pharmacotherapy of disruptive behavior disorders in children and adolescents. *Psychopharmacology, 191*(1), 127–140. doi:10.1007/s00213-006-0537-6

Jacobson, L. (2008). Teacher-pupil link crucial to pre-k success, study says. *Education Week, 27*(38), 9.

James, J., Ellis, B. J., Schlomer, G. L., & Garber, J. (2012). Sex-specific pathways to early puberty, sexual debut, and sexual risk taking: Tests of an integrated evolutionary–developmental model. *Developmental psychology, 48*, 687–702.

Kazdin, A. E., Siegel, T. C., & Bass, D. (1992). Cognitive problem-solving skills training and parent management training in the treatment of antisocial behavior in children. *Journal of Consulting and Clinical Psychology, 60*(5), 733–747. doi:10.1037/0022-006X.60.5.733

Khanna, D., Shaw, J., Dolan, M., & Lennox, C. (2014). Does diagnosis affect the predictive accuracy of risk assessment tools for juvenile offenders: Conduct Disorder and Attention Deficit Hyperactivity Disorder. *Journal of Adolescence* [serial online], *37*(7), 1171–1179. doi:10.1016/j.adolescence.2014.08.008

Knoff, H. M. (2002, March). The "Stop and Think!" Social Skills Program: Teaching children interpersonal and conflict resolution skills systems. *NASP Communiqué, 30*, 18–19.

Kolko, D. J., Herschell, A. D., & Scharf, D. M. (2006). Education and treatment for boys who set fires: specificity, moderators, and predictors of recidivism. *Journal of Emotional & Behavioral Disorders, 14*(4), 227–239.

Kruesi, M. J. P., Casanova, M. F., Mannheim, G., & Johnson-Bilder, A. J. (2004). Reduced temporal lobe volume in early onset conduct disorder. *Neuroimaging, 132*(1), 1–11.

Lahey, B. B., Goodman, S. H., Waldman, I. D., Bird, H., Canino, G., Jensen, P., . . . Applegate, B. (1999). Relation of age of onset to the type and severity of child and adolescent conduct problems. *Journal of Abnormal Child Psychology, 27*(4), 247–260. doi:10.1023/A:1022661224769

Leong, F. L., & Gupta, A. (2008). Culture and race in counseling and psychotherapy: A critical review of the literature. In S. D. Brown, R. W. Lent, S. D. Brown, & R. W. Lent (Eds.), *Handbook of counseling psychology* (4th ed., pp. 320–337). Hoboken, NJ: John Wiley & Sons.

Linehan, M. (1993). *Cognitive behavioral treatment of borderline personality disorder.* New York, NY: The Guilford Press.

Lochman, J. E., Powell, N., Boxmeyer, C., Andrade, B., Stromeyer, S. L., & Jimenez-Camargo, L. A. (2012). Adaptations to the coping power program's structure, delivery settings, and clinician training. *Psychotherapy,* 49(2), 135–142. doi:10.1037/a0027165

Lochman, J. E., & Wells, K. C. (2002). Contextual social-cognitive mediators and child outcome: A test of the theoretical model in the Coping Power Program. *Development and Psychopathology, 14*, 945–967.

Matuschek, T., Jaeger, S., Stadelmann, S., Dölling, K., Grunewald, M., Weis, S., . . . Döhnert, M. (2016). Implementing the K-SADS-PL as a standard diagnostic tool: Effects on clinical diagnoses. *Psychiatry Research, 236,* 119–124. doi:10.1016/j.psychres.2015.12.021

McCabe, K. M., Hough, R., Wood, P. A., & Yeh, M. (2001). Childhood and adolescent onset conduct disorder: A test of the developmental taxonomy. *Journal of Abnormal Child Psychology, 29*(4), 305–316.

McKinney, E., Bartholomew, C., & Gray, L. (2010). RTI and SWPBIS: Confronting the problem of disproportionality. *The Communique, 38*(6). Retrieved from www.nasponline.org/publications/periodicals/communique/issues/volume-38-issue-6/rti-and-swpbis-confronting-the-problem-of-disproportionality

McLaughlin, K. A., Green, J. G., Hwang, I., Sampson, N. A., Zaslavsky, A. M., & Kessler, R. C. (2012). Intermittent explosive disorder in the National Comorbidity Survey Replication Adolescent Supplement. *JAMA Psychiatry, 69*(11), 1131–1139.

Mehler-Wex, C., Romanos, M., & Warnke, A. (2014). Aggressive and autoaggressive behavior, impulse control disorder, and conduct disorder. In M. Gerlach, A. Warnke, & L. Greenhill (Eds.), *Psychiatric drugs in children and adolescents: Basic pharmacology and practical applications* (pp. 337–350). New York, NY: Springer-Verlag Publishing. doi:10.1007/978-3-7091-1501-5

Millon, T. (1993). *Million adolescent clinical inventory manual.* Minneapolis, MN: National Computer Systems.

Millon, T., & Davis, R. D. (1993). The Millon Adolescent Personality Inventory and the Millon Adolescent Clinical Inventory. *Journal Of Counseling & Development, 71*(5), 570-574. doi:10.1002/j.1556-6676.1993.tb02244.x

Moffitt, T. E. (2003). Life-course-persistent and adolescence-limited antisocial behavior: A 10-year research review and a research agenda. In B. B. Lahey, T. E. Moffitt, & A. Caspi (Eds.), *Causes of conduct disorder and juvenile delinquency* (pp. 49–75). New York, NY: The Guilford Press.

Moffitt, T. E., Caspi, A., Dickson, N., Silva, P., & Stanton, W. (1996). Childhood-onset versus adolescent-onset antisocial conduct problems in males: Natural history from ages 3 to 18 years. *Developmental and Psychopathology, 8*(2), 399–424.

Muratori, P., Lochman, J. E., Manfredi, A., Milone, A., Nocentini, A., Pisano, S., & Masi, G. (2016). Callous unemotional traits in children with disruptive behavior disorder: Predictors of developmental trajectories and adolescent outcomes. *Psychiatry Research, 236,* 35–41. doi:10.1016/j.psychres.2016.01.003

Myers, M. G., Stewart, D. G., & Brown, S. A. (1998). Progression from conduct disorder to antisocial personality disorder following treatment for adolescent substance abuse. *The American Journal of Psychiatry, 155*(4), 479–485.

Nance, J. P. (2016) Dismantling the school-to-prison pipeline: Tools for change. *Arizona State Law Journal, 48*(2), 313–372.

National Association of School Psychologists. (2001). *Zero tolerance and alternative strategies: A fact sheet for educators and policymakers.* Retrieved from www .nasponline.org/resources/factsheets/zt_fs.aspx

Nevels, R. M., Dehon, E. E., Alexander, K., & Gontkovsky, S. T. (2010). Psychopharmacology of aggression in children and adolescents with primary neuropsychiatric disorders: A review of current and potentially promising treatment options. *Experimental and Clinical Psychopharmacology, 18*(2), 184–201.

Niec, L. N., Barnett, M. L., Prewett, M. S., & Shanley Chatham, J. R. (2016). Group parent–child interaction therapy: A randomized control trial for the treatment of conduct problems in young children. *Journal of Consulting and Clinical Psychology, 84*(8), 682–698. doi:10.1037/a0040218

Nock, M. K., Kazdin, A. E., Hiripi, E., & Kessler, R. C. (2006) Prevalence, subtypes, and correlates of DSM-IV conduct disorder in the National Comorbidity Survey Replication. *Psychological Medicine, 36*(5), 699–710.

Nock, M. K., Kazdin, A. E., Hiripi, E., & Kessler, R. C. (2007) Lifetime prevalence, correlates, and persistence of oppositional defiant disorder: Results from the National Comorbidity Survey Replication. *Journal of Child Psychology & Psychiatry, 48*(7), 703–713. doi:10.1111/j.1469-7610.2007.01733.x.

Office of Special Education Program (OSEP) Center on PBIS, United States Department of Education. (2010, September 25). *Implementation blueprint and self-assessment positive behavioral interventions and supports.* Retrieved from www.pbis.org/common/cms/files/pbisresources/SWPBS_Implementation Blueprint_vSep_23_2010.pdf

Olfson, M., King, M., & Schoenbaum, M. (2015). Treatment of young people with antipsychotic medications in the United States. *JAMA Psychiatry, 72*(9), 867–874. doi:10.1001/jamapsychiatry.2015.0500.

Oliver, D. G., Caldwell, C. H., Faison, N., Sweetman, J. A., Abelson, J. M., & Jackson, J. S. (2016). Prevalence of DSM-IV intermittent explosive disorder in Black adolescents: Findings from the National Survey of American Life, Adolescent Supplement. *American Journal of Orthopsychiatry, 86*(5), 552–563. doi:10.1037/ort0000170

Ortega, L., Lyubansky, M., Nettles, S., & Espelage, D. L. (2016). Outcomes of a restorative circles program in a high school setting. *Psychology of Violence, 6*(3), 459–468. doi:10.1037/vio0000048

Papazoglou, A., Jacobson, L. A., McCabe, M., Kaufmann, W., & Zabel, T. A. (2014). To ID or not to ID? Changes in classification rates of intellectual disability using DSM-5. *Intellectual and Developmental Disabilities, 52*(3), 165–174. doi:10.1352/1934-9556-52.3.165

Patterson, D. A., Dulmus, C. N., Maguin, E., & Perkins, J. (2016) Differential outcomes in agency-based mental health care between minority and majority youth. *Research on Social Work Practice, 26*(3), 260–265.

Piotrowska, P. J., Stride, C. B., Croft, S. E., & Rowe, R. (2015). Socioeconomic status and antisocial behaviour among children and adolescents: A systematic review and meta-analysis. *Clinical Psychology Review, 35,* 47–55. doi:10.1016/j.cpr.2014.11.003

Practice parameter for the assessment and treatment of children and adolescents with oppositional defiant disorder. (2007). *Journal of the American Academy of Child & Adolescent Psychiatry, 46*(1), 126–141. doi:10.1097/01.chi.0000246060.62706.af

Practice parameter for the assessment and treatment of children and adolescents with reactive attachment disorder of infancy and early childhood. (2005). *Journal of the American Academy of Child & Adolescent Psychiatry, 44*(11), 1206–1219. doi:10.1097/01.chi.0000177056.41655.ce

Prentky, R., & Righthand, S. (2003). *Juvenile Sex Offender Assessment Protocol-II (J-SOAP-II) manual.* Washington, DC: U.S. Department of Justice, Office of Justice Programs, Office of Juvenile Justice and Delinquency Prevention.

Rescorla, L. A., Bochicchio, L., Achenbach, T. M., Ivanova, M. Y., Almqvist, F., Begovac, I., . . . Verhulst, F. C. (2014). Parent–teacher agreement on children's problems in 21 societies. *Journal of Clinical Child and Adolescent Psychology, 43*(4), 627–642. doi:10.1080/15374416.2014.900719

Reynolds, C., & Kamphaus, R. (2015). *The behavior assessment system for children* (3rd ed.). San Antonio, TX: Pearson publishing. Retrieved from www.pearsonclinical.com/education/products/100001402/behavior-assessment-system-for-children-third-edition-basc-3.html?cmpid=300219-PPC-BASC3&gclid=CNfy66n54csCFUxZhgodM48Bdw#tab-details

Rhee, S. H., & Waldman, I. D. (2002). Genetic and environmental influences on antisocial behavior: A meta-analysis of twin and adoption studies. *Psychological Bulletin, 128*(3), 490–529.

Richters, M. M., & Volkmar, F. (1994), Reactive attachment disorder of infancy or early childhood. *Journal of the American Academy of Child and Adolescent Psychiatry, 33,* 328–332.

Robbins, M. S., Alexander, J. F., Turner, C. W., & Hollimon, A. (2016). Evolution of functional family therapy as an evidence-based practice for adolescents with disruptive behavior problems. *Family Process,* doi:10.1111/famp.12230.

Rones, M., & Hoagwood, K. (2000). School-based mental health services: A research review. *Clinical, Child and Family Psychology Review, 3*(4), 223–241

Salekin, R. T. (2015, September 21). Psychopathy in childhood: Toward better informing the DSM-5 and ICD-11 conduct disorder specifiers. *Personality*

Disorders: Theory, Research, and Treatment. Advance online publication. doi:10.1037/per0000150

Sawyer, A. M., Borduin, C. M., & Dopp, A. R. (2015). Long-term effects of prevention and treatment on youth antisocial behavior: A meta-analysis. *Clinical Psychology Review, 42,* 130–144. doi:10.1016/j.cpr.2015.06.009

Sebastian, C. L., DeBrito, S. A., McCrory, E. J., Hyde, Z. H., Lockwood, P. L., Cecil C. A., & Viding, E. (2016). Grey matter volumes in children with conduct problems and varying levels of callous-unemotional traits. *Journal of Abnormal Child Psychology, 44*(4), 639–649.

The Sentencing Project. (2015, December 15). *Trends in US corrections.* Retrieved from www.sentencingproject.org/publications/trends-in-u-s-corrections/

Simmel, C., Brooks, D., Barth, R. P., & Hinshaw, S. P. (2001). Externalizing symptomatology among adoptive youth: Prevalence and preadoption risk factors. *Journal of Abnormal Child Psychology, 29*(1), 57–69. doi:10.1023/A:1005251513130

Skiba, R. (2000). *Zero tolerance, zero evidence: An analysis of school disciplinary practice* (Policy Research Report No. SRS2). Bloomington, IN: Indiana Education Policy Center. Retrieved from http://ceep.indiana.edu/ChildrenLeft-Behind/pdf/ZeroTolerance.pdf

Skiba, R. (2014) The failure of zero tolerance. *Reclaiming Children & Youth,* 22(4), 27–33.

Steinberg, L. (2014) *Age of opportunity: Lessons from the new science of adolescence.* New York, NY: Houghton Mifflin Harcourt.

Steiner, H., & Remsing, L. (2007). Practice parameter for the assessment and treatment of children and adolescents with oppositional defiant disorder. *Journal of the American Academy of Child & Adolescent Psychiatry, 46*(1), 126–141. doi:10.1097/01.chi.0000246060.62706.af

Sterzer, P., Stadler, C., Poustaka, F., & Kleinschmidt, A. (2007) A structural neural deficit in adolescents with conduct disorder and its association with lack of empathy. *Neuroimage, 37*(1), 335–342.

Stevens, M. C., & Haney-Caron, E. (2012). Comparison of brain volume abnormalities between ADHD and conduct disorder in adolescence. *Journal of Psychiatry and Neuroscience, 37*(6), 389–398.

Substance Abuse and Mental Health Services Administration. (2015). Retrieved from www.samhsa.gov/disorders/mental

Sutton, L. R., Hughes, T. L., Huang, A., Lehman, C., Paserba, D., Talkington, V., . . . Marshall, S. (2013). Identifying individuals with autism in a state facility for adolescents adjudicated as sexual offenders: A pilot study. *Focus on Autism and other Developmental Disabilities, 28*(3), 175–183. doi:10.1177/1088357612462060

Tallichet, S. E., & Hensley, C. (2004). Exploring the link between recurrent acts of childhood and adolescent animal cruelty and subsequent violent crime. *Criminal Justice Review, 29*(2), 304–316. doi:10.1177/073401680402900203

Tervalon, M., & Murray-Garcia, J. (1998). Cultural humility versus cultural competence: A critical distinction in defining physician training outcomes in multicultural education. *Journal of Health Care for the Poor and Underserved, 9*, 117–125.

Wakefield, J., Pottick, K. J., & Kirk, S. A., (2002). Should the DSM-IV diagnostic criteria for conduct disorder consider social context? *The American Journal of Psychiatry, 159*(3), 380–386. doi:10.1176/appi.ajp.159.3.380

Washburn, J. J., Romero, E. G., Welty, L. J., Abram, K. M., Teplin, L. A., McClelland, G. M., & Paskar, L. D. (2007). Development of antisocial personality disorder in detained youths: The predictive value of mental disorders. *Journal of Consulting and Clinical Psychology, 75*(2), 221–231. doi:10.1037/0022-006X.75.2.221.

Watson, T. S., Gresham, F. M., & Skinner, C. H. (2001). Introduction to the mini-series: Issues and procedures for implementing functional behavior assessments in schools. *School Psychology Review, 30*(2), 153–155.

Webster-Stratton, C., & Reid, M. J. (2007). Incredible years parents and teachers training series: A head start partnership to promote social competence and prevent conduct problems. In P. Tolan, J. Szapocznik & S. Sambrano, (Eds.), *Preventing youth substance abuse: Science-based programs for children and adolescents* (pp. 67–88). Washington, DC: American Psychological Association. doi:10.1037/11488-003

Webster-Stratton, C., Rinaldi, J., & Reid, J. M. (2011). Long-term outcomes of Incredible Years parenting program: Predictors of adolescent adjustment. *Child and Adolescent Mental Health, 16*(1), 38–46. doi:10.1111/j.1475-3588.2010.00576.x

Whitaker, A., & Rao, U. (1992). Neuroleptics in pediatric psychiatry. *Psychiatric Clinics of North America, 15*(1), 243–276.

White, S. F., Frick, P. J., Lawing, K., & Bauer, D. (2013). Callous–unemotional traits and response to functional family therapy in adolescent offenders. *Behavioral Sciences & The Law, 31*(2), 271–285. doi:10.1002/bsl.2041

Wiesner, M., Windle, M., Kanouse, D. E., Elliott, M. N., & Schuster, M. A. (2015). DISC Predictive Scales (DPS): Factor structure and uniform differential item functioning across gender and three racial/ethnic groups for ADHD, conduct disorder, and oppositional defiant disorder symptoms. *Psychological Assessment, 27*(4), 1324–1336. doi:10.1037/pas000010

Woolgar, M., & Baldock, E. (2015). Attachment disorders versus more common problems in looked after and adopted children: Comparing community and expert assessments. *Child and Adolescent Mental Health, 20*(1), 34–40. doi:10.1111/camh.12052

Woolgar, M., & Scott, S. (2014). The negative consequences of over-diagnosing attachment disorders in adopted children: The importance of comprehensive formulations. *Clinical Child Psychology and Psychiatry, 19*(3), 355–366. doi:10.1177/1359104513478545

Woolley, J. (1997). Thinking about fantasy: Are children fundamentally different thinkers from adults? *Child Development, 68*(6), 991–1011.

Worling, J. R., & Curwen, T. (2000). *The ERASOR: Estimate of risk of adolescent sexual offence recidivism.* Toronto, ON: SAFE-T Program, Thistletown Regional Centre.

Zirkel, P. A. (2011). State special education laws for functional behavioral assessment and behavior intervention plans. *Behavioral Disorders, 36*(4), 262–278.

Zisser, A., & Eyberg, S. E. (2010). Parent child interaction therapy and the treatment of disruptive behavior disorders. In J. R. Weisz & A. E. Kazdin (Eds.), *Evidence-based psychotherapies for children and adolescents* (2nd ed., pp. 179–193). New York, NY: The Guilford Press.

Index

OTHER TITLES IN OUR CHILD CLINICAL PSYCHOLOGY "NUTS AND BOLTS" COLLECTION

Samuel T. Gontkovsky, *Editor*

- *Learning Disabilities* by Charles J. Golden and Lisa K. Lashley
- *Intellectual Disabilities* by Charles J. Golden and Lisa K. Lashley
- *A Guide for Statistics in the Behavioral Sciences* by Jeff Foster
- *Childhood Sleep Disorders* by Connie J. Schnoes
- *Childhood and Adolescent Obesity* by Lauren A Stutts
- *Elimination Disorders: Evidence-Based Treatment for Enuresis and Encopresis* by Thomas M. Reimers
- *Depression in Childhood and Adolescence: A Guide for Practitioners* by Rebecca A. Schwartz-Mette, Cynthia A. Erdley, Douglas W. Nangle and Hannah Lawrence
- *Childhood Anxiety Disorders* by Ashley J. Smith and Amy M. Jacobsen

Momentum Press offers over 30 collections including Aerospace, Biomedical, Civil, Environmental, Nanomaterials, Geotechnical, and many others. We are a leading book publisher in the field of engineering, mathematics, health, and applied sciences.

Momentum Press is actively seeking collection editors as well as authors. For more information about becoming an MP author or collection editor, please visit http://www.momentumpress.net/contact

Announcing Digital Content Crafted by Librarians

Concise e-books business students need for classroom and research

Momentum Press offers digital content as authoritative treatments of advanced engineering topics by leaders in their field. Hosted on ebrary, MP provides practitioners, researchers, faculty, and students in engineering, science, and industry with innovative electronic content in sensors and controls engineering, advanced energy engineering, manufacturing, and materials science.

Momentum Press offers library-friendly terms:
- *perpetual access for a one-time fee*
- *no subscriptions or access fees required*
- *unlimited concurrent usage permitted*
- *downloadable PDFs provided*
- *free MARC records included*
- *free trials*

The **Momentum Press** digital library is very affordable, with no obligation to buy in future years.

For more information, please visit **www.momentumpress.net/library** or to set up a trial in the US, please contact **mpsales@globalepress.com**.

www.ingramcontent.com/pod-product-compliance
Lightning Source LLC
Chambersburg PA
CBHW050536270326
41926CB00015B/3255